Mindful Learning

101 **Proven Strategies for Student and Teacher Success**

Mindful Learning

101 **Proven Strategies for Student and Teacher Success**

Linda Campbell

CORWIN PRESS, INC.
A Sage Publications Company
Thousand Oaks, California

For information:

Corwin Press, Inc.
A Sage Publications Company
2455 Teller Road
Thousand Oaks, California 91320
www.corwinpress.com

Sage Publications Ltd.
6 Bonhill Street
London EC2A 4PU
United Kingdom

Sage Publications India Pvt. Ltd.
B-42, Panchsheel Enclave
Post Box 4109
New Delhi 110 017 India

Printed in the United States of America

Library of Congress Cataloging-in-Publication Data

Campbell, Linda, 1948-
Mindful learning:101 strategies for student and teacher success / Linda Campbell.
    p. cm.
Includes bibliographical references and index.
ISBN 0-7619-4571-7 (C) — ISBN 0-7619-4572-5 (P) 1. Effective teaching—United States.
2. Cognitive styles in children—United States. 3. Individual differences in children—
United States. 4. Learning strategies—United States. I. Title: One hundred one strategies for
mindful learning. II. Title: One hundred and one strategies for mindful learning.
III. Title.
LB1025.3 .C34 2003
371.102—dc21   2002012368

This book is printed on acid-free paper.

03 04 05 06 10 9 8 7 6 5 4 3 2

cover

Editor-at-Large:	Mark Goldberg
Acquisitions Editor:	Faye Zucker
Editorial Assistant:	Julia Parnell
Copy Editor:	Hawley Roddick
Production Editor:	Diane S. Foster
Typesetter:	C&M Digitals (P) Ltd.
Proofreader:	Olivia Weber
Indexer:	Teri Greenberg
Cover Designer:	Tracy E. Miller
Production Designer:	Janet Foulger

Contents

3. Ensuring Gender-Fair Instruction: For Female and Male Students

Acknowledgments

This book would not exist without the gentle nudging of my editor, Mark Goldberg. Thank you, Mark, for seeing this work through to its completion. Likewise, I am grateful that Corwin Press found this book worthy of publication. I am daily indebted to the love and support of my husband Bruce and my son, Daniel Misch. Though they are rarely acknowledged, I am grateful to educational researchers and their work that informs and inspires us all.

This book is dedicated to teachers everywhere
because their work matters so much to everyone.

About the Author

Linda Campbell, PhD, is Professor of Education at Antioch University Seattle. She is also the Project Director of the Early College High School Initiative for Native Youth funded by the Bill and Melinda Gates Foundation, the Kellogg Foundation, the Ford Foundation, and the Carnegie Corporation of New York. Previously, she served as a public school teacher for 12 years at the K-12 levels. She has also authored numerous articles, chapters, and books, including the best seller *Teaching and Learning Through Multiple Intelligences*. In addition to serving as a National Education Association school restructuring specialist, consultant, and presenter, she works with schools to promote the high school and college retention and achievement of Native American youth. She may be reached by email at lcampbell@antiochsea.edu.

CORWIN
PRESS

The Corwin Press logo—a raven striding across an open book—represents the happy union of courage and learning. We are a professional-level publisher of books and journals for K-12 educators, and we are committed to creating and providing resources that embody these qualities. Corwin's motto is "Success for All Learners."

Introduction

This book puts ready-to-use instructional strategies into the hands of teachers. Rather than being just a compendium of good ideas for the classroom, the techniques here have been *proven* to strengthen student achievement. Research shows a direct link between how students are taught and how well they achieve. In times of heightened accountability and increasing student diversity, teachers need, and fortunately have, new tools to improve instruction.

Historically, research has played a small role in decision making about teaching methods. Over the years, however, a knowledge base has emerged of specific strategies that yield consistent results with many teachers and students. This book taps into that literature. Education is poised to become a research-based profession. Solid and reliable knowledge can enhance the quality of learning for all students.

As an experienced K–12 teacher and teacher educator, I have encountered scores of innovative theories and reform movements. I have witnessed how exciting ideas can leap from the pages of a new book or from the words of an inspirational presenter into mainstream practice, with little attention paid to the actual impact on student performance. Frequently, such concepts spread unabated through classrooms, schools, and, in some cases, the country. When educational innovations do not deliver as promised, teachers often are held responsible for the lackluster results. In reality, they were given little to work with in the first place.

Recently, several researchers have observed the phenomenon of theory- or fad-driven educational change. They have noted, too, that innovations in classroom methods are rarely researched at length (Diamond & Hopson, 1998, citing Stigler & Bruer; Ellis & Fouts, 1997; Grossen, 2000). By skipping over instruction, the heart and soul of any improvement effort is neglected and the effort is unlikely to succeed.

To correct this oversight, this book compiles 101 research-substantiated, *mindful* instructional strategies. In this book, being mindful means using proven classroom practices that have worked on other occasions and are most likely to work again. It means making informed, professional decisions about how best to teach, and it means balancing enthusiasm and personal opinion with research-based strategies so that consistent results are realized.

The suggestion of basing one's practice upon research does not imply that teachers should never innovate. There will be times in every classroom when teachers and students will work autonomously, but it is also true that there will be many occasions when research-tested practices will boost student learning the most. It is also important to note that great strides in achievement won't occur just from loving teaching. We expect doctors, mechanics, pilots, and architects to do more than love their work. Each relies on professional knowledge to attain predictable results. Being mindful as teachers means putting our professional knowledge base to effective use. We can combine love with knowledge and skill to make American education the best in the world.

Where did the techniques in this book come from, and why were they chosen? Readers should know that the book's 101 strategies were derived from two primary sources: the cognitive sciences and researched instructional practices. The cognitive sciences influenced the selection of categories in this book: background knowledge, student diversity, and active learning. Within these categories, several instructional strategies are described. The research that warrants their inclusion in classroom practice is explained. Every strategy in this book has worked in real classrooms.

THE NEW SCIENCE OF LEARNING

The last four decades have witnessed a revolution in the study of the human mind. In the late 1950s, a new, multidisciplinary field emerged, that of the cognitive sciences (Bransford, Brown, & Cocking, 1999; Diamond & Hopson, 1998; Gardner, 1985). Made up of psychology, linguistics, philosophy, computer science, neuroscience, and anthropology, the cognitive sciences have delved into the complexity of thinking and learning. Much of the research on learning comes from studies of the development of expertise, the acquisition and transfer of knowledge, problem solving, and teaching effectiveness. We have learned about the physiological, cultural, metacognitive, emotional, interpersonal, and dispositional aspects of learning and, while much of this research is new, it has not yet explored the depths of human cognition.

This is mentioned not to discount this book but rather to situate it in the context of what is known about learning at this time. In so doing, sensationalized claims such as those currently made about the mind and, in particular, its home, the human brain, can be avoided.

I agree with Sylwester (1995), a noted author in brain research and education, who reminded educators of our tendency to advocate for unproven methodologies. He wrote, "We've already demonstrated our vulnerability with the educational spillover of the split brain research: the right brain/left brain books, workshops, and curricular programs whose recommendations went far beyond the research findings" (p. 6). Likewise, brain researchers themselves echo such thoughts. LeDoux (*Education Commission of the States*, 1996), an authority on the neuroscientific basis of emotion, observed, "These ideas are easy to sell to the public, but it is easy to take them beyond their actual basis in science" (p. 5). Miller (1993), asserted, "It will be years, perhaps centuries, before we come up against the 'cognitive' closure" (p. 138).

Essentially, all learning is brain based. As with any complex issue, there have been oversimplifications and misrepresentations of what is actually known and how educators should proceed. Likewise, in today's literature, the words *brain* and *mind* are often used interchangeably. Emerging research is intriguing, and, eventually, educators will have solid information upon which to base all professional practice. However, at this time, it appears that there are too few studies on the educational implications of brain research to offer any reliable support for specific reforms (Bransford, Brown, & Cocking, 1999; Damasio & Damasio, 1993; Ellis & Fouts, 1997; Sylwester, 1995). Instead, brain research is one facet of the new science of learning which informs this book, the important research on effective instructional practices. Again, I am interested in placing in the hands of teachers strategies that have actually worked in classrooms.

BEST PRACTICES

Best practice is another educational concept that has been used widely without reference to any solid knowledge base. Not wanting to put readers in a position of simply having to take my word for the effectiveness of the strategies in this book, I have searched the literature for research-tested practices that actually resulted in student achievement gains. What literature did I use? The majority of the 101 strategies were pulled from three sources: (a) the instructional processes used by high-performing teachers and high-performing schools, (b) research metaanalyses of instructional techniques, and (c) research studies. Extensive reference lists are offered at the end of each chapter for readers who are interested in accessing these resources themselves. Additionally, each chapter begins with a brief review of the literature and the rationale for the inclusion of each strategy.

Readers should be aware that not all the techniques in this book are new. While reform movements tend to emphasize cutting-edge initiatives, contributions from old researched techniques are also noteworthy. As our knowledge base about effective teaching grows, it should integrate worthwhile discoveries from the past. It is unlikely that many in medicine would shun the Salk vaccine and risk an outbreak of polio simply because the research occurred decades ago.

As the reader peruses this book, a word of caution is in order. I do not mean to imply that each technique will yield substantial achievement gains in every classroom. What I am saying is that research can identify which teaching practices are most likely to produce the desired results. The book's 101 strategies were selected, in part, as a reaction against educational fads that come and go with little to justify their presence. At the same time, I am well aware that research does not necessarily capture all that is valuable in teaching and learning. There may be enhanced attitudes, values, and process of engagement that studies overlook but that readers and their students may encounter when participating in new learning approaches.

WHAT THIS BOOK INCLUDES

The content and format of this book were carefully considered. An array of practices are offered for the range of aptitudes, interests, and diversity of students in contemporary classrooms in a simple, numbered, easy-to-access format. Both research and instructional practices are featured in each chapter. One strategy is described per page, or, in some cases, multiple examples of an individual strategy are given. While the literature base that supports the inclusion of the techniques can be read in a short time, annotated resources are included in each chapter and references are at the back of the book, for those who desire additional information. It should be noted that instead of treating the metacognitive processes of higher-level thinking and problem-solving skills separately, I have integrated them into the strategies included in this book.

As mentioned earlier, research from the cognitive sciences guided the focus of this book's three broad topics: prior knowledge, active learning, and student diversity. Chapter 1 summarizes the research on prior learning and suggests 15 instructional approaches for enlisting background knowledge to improve student learning. Chapter 2 reviews three different approaches to active learning in the classroom. The 30 strategies in this chapter are split among three areas: whole-to-part or big-picture learning, multimodal learning, and content-specific instruction. Chapter 3 discusses the gender-related research on student achievement and outlines 20 instructional approaches to enhance the achievement of both males and females. Chapter 4 underscores the need to respond to the diversity among our students. Its 20 mindful strategies are divided among culture's influence on learning, limited English proficiency issues, the role of socioeconomic class and learning, and inclusive classroom approaches. Chapter 5 discusses new initiatives in performance-based assessment and provides 16 strategies for documenting classroom achievement.

THE QUESTION THIS BOOKS ANSWERS

This book responds to the question, "How can I make my teaching more effective?" The 101 techniques have proven track records with female and male students and with students of diverse ages, languages, abilities, and socioeconomic status. Teachers of every grade and subject will find strategies to apply or adapt to their circumstances. I recognize that teachers may have to adjust the level of a strategy to fit Grade 1 or 4 or 9, but teachers are good at that when they have clear material. I also understand that no one can use all 101 strategies or do all that I recommend all the time. Teachers are encouraged to focus on those strategies of particular importance to them and appropriate for their classrooms.

Ultimately, effective teachers grow by becoming lifelong students of learning. Part of being a student of learning includes knowing how and why certain strategies work in the classroom. Just as we endeavor to teach students important skills, knowledge, and attitudes, we can model such skills, attitudes, and knowledge ourselves by using research to guide our efforts. Today, as challenges and demands increase both inside and outside the classroom, so has the available research on what works. One teacher in one classroom when supported with effective instructional strategies can make a profound difference in the lives of students.

REFERENCES

Bransford, J. D., Brown, A. L., & Cocking, R. R. (Eds.). (1999). *How people learn: Brain, mind, experience, and school.* Washington, DC: National Academy Press.

Damasio, A. R., & Damasio, H. (1993). Brain and language. *Scientific American. Mind and Brain* (pp. 54-65). New York: W. H. Freeman.

Diamond, M., & Hopson, J. (1998). *Magic trees of the mind: How to nurture your child's intelligence, creativity, and healthy emotions from birth through adolescence.* New York: Penguin.

Education Commission of the States. (1996). *Bridging the gap between neuroscience and education.* Denver, CO: Author.

Ellis, A. K., & Fouts, J. T. (1997). *Research on educational innovations.* Larchmont, NY: Eye on Education.

Gardner, H. (1985). *The mind's new science: A history of the cognitive revolution.* New York: Basic Books.

Grossen, B. (2000). *What does it mean to be a research-based profession?* Retrieved August 2, 2002, from University of Oregon, darkwing.uoregon.edu/~bgrossen/pubs/resprf.htm

Miller, J. (1993). Trouble in mind. *Scientific American. Mind and Brain.* (pp. 137-138). New York: W. H. Freeman.

Sylwester, R. (1995). *A celebration of neurons: An educator's guide to the human brain.* Alexandria, VA: Association for Supervision and Curriculum Development.

1

Beginning With What Students Know

Activating Prior Knowledge

You've probably watched televised ice skating competitions and heard announcers wax rhapsodic about double axles or triple Lutzes. Perhaps the distinctions among these skating feats escaped you. Unless the announcer explained the movements or you figured them out for yourself, it is likely your confusion remained during and after the competition.

This experience is reenacted in our classrooms daily. Many students lack adequate prior knowledge to extract meaning from our instruction. Yet we often make assumptions that they come to class possessing the skills and information to learn what we teach. Some research suggests that this assumption is erroneous and that learning is influenced as much by students' prior knowledge as by the new instruction they receive. Attention needs to be paid to this fundamental aspect of the learning process.

Students, of any age, bring beliefs and life and academic experiences to the classroom that influence what and how they learn. At times, such prior knowledge facilitates learning by creating mental hooks that serve to anchor instructional concepts. Conversely, the acquisition of new content can be thwarted if it conflicts with students' preexisting misinformation. As a result, the role of prior knowledge in learning is paradoxical: It can lead to success and failure in the classroom. Consequently, teachers and students alike can benefit from taking time before instruction to identify what is known or, more accurately, believed to be known about a topic. Many strategies can tap students' prior knowledge. Later in this chapter, several are described.

WHAT ROLE DOES BACKGROUND KNOWLEDGE PLAY IN LEARNING?

Piaget (1968) disagreed with the *tabula rasa* notion of the child's mind. Instead, he proposed that young children gradually developed cognitive structures to make sense of the world. By the time they enter school, students have constructed informal theories about how things work, about themselves, and about others (Carey & Gelman, 1991; Gardner, 1991). One example of a common childhood theory is the distinction between living and nonliving things. Some children perceive movement as a way to distinguish what is alive and what isn't. Since people move, they are alive, while plants are not, because they are stationary. In the classroom, children's conceptions about living and nonliving categories, or any other topic about to be taught, can be activated. When this is done, teaching shifts from transmitting knowledge to blank, absorbent minds to refining and restructuring preexisting notions. Gardner (1991) asserts that a significant purpose of education is to correct erroneous notions children develop early in life.

When preparing for instruction, most of us focus tremendous effort on the content we will teach. Little planning and instructional time is dedicated to accessing preexisting knowledge. This oversight can have significant implications. If students' preexisting knowledge conflicts with the presented material, the new information risks being distorted. For example, studies at all grade levels have shown students' chronic misunderstanding of basic physics concepts. When they attempt to explain the upward toss of a ball, they describe an initial upward force that is balanced at the top of its trajectory, and pulled by gravity back to the earth (Roschelle, 1997).

Physicists, by contrast, explain the ball toss in terms of a single force, that of gravity with positive, zero, and decreasing momentum. Research has shown that errors in solving math and science problems are not random (Roschelle, 1997). Instead, they emerge from students' underlying concepts or homespun theories. Furthermore, when students are asked to produce rote memory answers to questions, they may appear to know more than they do. If asked to apply the concepts to new problems or to give analogies, they may give responses that consist of unconventional and unacceptable explanations. To counteract the potential negative influence of prior knowledge, teachers and students can dedicate time and effort to making thinking visible and malleable.

It would be a mistake to think that prior knowledge's only influence on learning is negative. This is not the case. All learning ultimately begins with the known and proceeds to the unknown. Background knowledge is the raw material that conditions learning. It serves as a basic building block. In many instances, students possess relevant knowledge that can assist them in successfully mastering new content. For example, most children have numerous informal methods for working with math in their everyday lives. This knowledge can be tapped when the formal symbol systems of addition and subtraction are taught in the classroom. By connecting everyday experiences with subjects encountered in school, students are likely to learn in lasting ways. Furthermore, by taking a few moments to activate prior knowledge, teachers demonstrate a respectful stance toward the wealth of ideas that all children possess when they walk into the classroom.

WHAT DO RESEARCH STUDIES SHOW ABOUT ACTIVATING PRIOR KNOWLEDGE?

Research has validated the role that activating prior knowledge plays in students' academic success. Many prior-knowledge studies have focused on the basic skills. For example, several studies have shown that reading comprehension increases when prior knowledge about the content of the text is activated (Christen & Murphy, 1991; Graves & Cook, 1980; Hayes & Tierney, 1982; Stevens, 1982). Successful techniques for activating background knowledge include using graphic organizers, asking questions about the topic, making associations, and using demonstrations or multimedia to enrich background knowledge. Such strategies are described later in this chapter.

Likewise, in science and math, studies reveal that activating prior knowledge assists in students' conceptual change. Clement, Brown, and Zeitsman (1989) developed a curriculum that elicited everyday knowledge to anchor and extend students' understanding of science concepts. Minstrell (1989) demonstrated the effectiveness of asking students questions about key concepts and clarifying them before studying scientific principles. Many studies have demonstrated that mathematics instruction should not necessarily begin with teaching computational algorithms but rather that students should explain their use of mathematics in everyday life (Ball, 1993; Carpenter & Fennema, 1992; Carpenter, Fennema, & Franke, 1996; Lambert, 1986).

In a metaanalysis of instructional strategies, Marzano (1998) found that simply asking students what they know about a topic before beginning a unit raises achievement. Additional worthwhile processes for eliciting prior knowledge include using visual representations, setting goals, comparing and contrasting with other knowledge, and giving brief explanations about the new content to be learned. Intentionally asking students questions before, during, and after a lesson involves them in retrieving what they already know.

Before instruction, it makes sense for teachers to tap what students might know about a topic. In general, students will exhibit one of three levels of prior knowledge. They might know *much*, *some*, or *little* about the content at hand. Perhaps students have relevant life experiences that shed light on the subject. Perhaps they have learned previous academic content that supports the new concept, and, in many cases, the topic might be unfamiliar or misinterpreted. Regardless of how much or little is known about a topic, teachers can diagnose student knowledge and fine-tune their instructional decisions based on what they learn. While there are innumerable ways to elicit prior knowledge, 15 research- and teacher-tested, mindful strategies follow for your classroom use.

#1: THE KNOWN AND THE UNKNOWN

Prepare a chart with two columns. Title the first column The Known and the second The Unknown (see Figure 1.1). Inform students of the topic they are about to study. To elicit their prior knowledge, ask open-ended questions about the concept. Sample questions might be, What makes stories interesting to read? or What makes plants grow? List responses in the first column of the chart. Concurrently, indicate areas where students exhibit little knowledge or confusion, and log these in the second column. Also ask students what piques their curiosity, and log their responses in the second column.

Figure 1.1 The Known and the Unknown

The Known	The Unknown

Known and Unknown charts can be saved or posted and referred to as students progress through a unit of study. Some teachers have students check off items as they learn them. Others put the charts away the day they are created and bring them out at the end of a unit for students to compare and contrast their prior and current content knowledge.

#2: THINGS I KNOW, THINK I KNOW, WANT TO KNOW

After specifying what students will study, ask them to brainstorm what they think they know and want to know about the topic. Make a chart and divide it into three sections titled, What I Know, What I Think I Know, and What I Want or Need to Know (K/T/WTK) (see Figure 1.2). List all suggested ideas. Ask contributors to identify the appropriate column for their suggestions.

Figure 1.2 K/T/WTK

What I Know	What I Think I Know	What I Want or Need to Know

SOURCE: Adapted from D. S. Ogle (1986).

#3: WHAT I KNOW, WANT TO KNOW, AND LEARNED

Three-column charts can be drawn that are similar to K/T/WTK, as shown in Figure 1.3. A teacher or student serving as the recorder can log what classmates say they already know about an upcoming lesson, what they want to know, and what they learned (KWL) after instruction. Although this method is similar to the one above, it differs in that it records the entire process of learning from prior knowledge to completed studies.

Figure 1.3 KWL

What I Know	What I Want to Know	What I Learned

SOURCE: Adapted from D. S. Ogle (1986).

#4: GETTING ORGANIZED GRAPHICALLY

Students' prior knowledge can be activated with simple graphic organizers. Graphic organizers are diagrams that visually display the relationships among ideas. They can assist students in organizing information and isolating important details. For the first example in Figure 1.4, students were asked to write a given topic in the center of a piece of paper (Step A). Next, they brainstormed topics they would like to pursue, as shown in Step B. As they progressed through the unit, they added to their organizers as shown in Step C.

Figure 1.4 Graphic Organizer

Step A:

Step B:

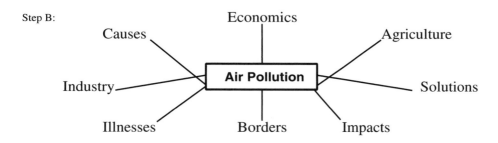

Step C:

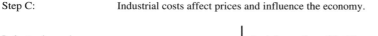

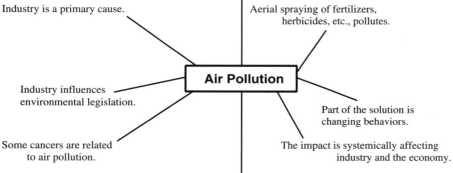

#5: VISUAL SEQUENCING

Background knowledge can be assessed or constructed by visually reviewing the steps of a lesson, a sequence of events, or a cyclical process. Two templates are provided in Figure 1.5: a flowchart and a cycle. At the beginning of a unit of study, students can be asked to identify an object, a procedure, or a critical event, and to specify its steps or stages—how one event leads to the next—and final outcomes. As they progress through their studies, students can correct earlier assumptions and elaborate on each component of a sequence or cycle.

Figure 1.5 Flowchart and Cycle

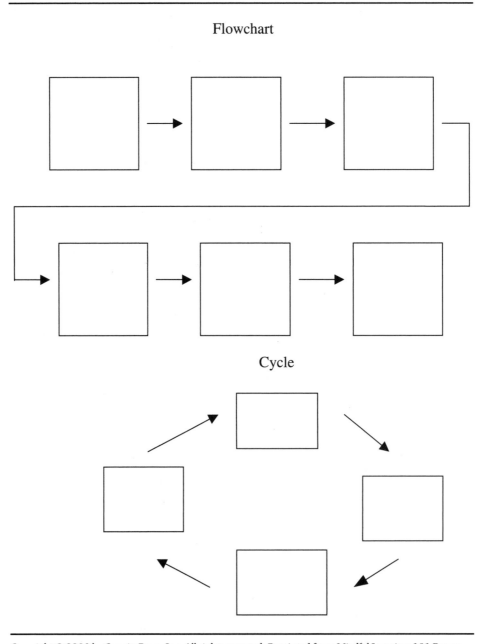

Flowchart

Cycle

#6: VISUALIZING CAUSE AND EFFECT

Students can be asked to explain their assumptions about the causes and effects of a particular event. Later, as they study the phenomena, they can compare and contrast their previous assumptions against what has been learned. Cause and effect charts (see Figure 1.6) are helpful when analyzing a social phenomenon, historical event, or scientific process.

Figure 1.6 Cause and Effect Chart

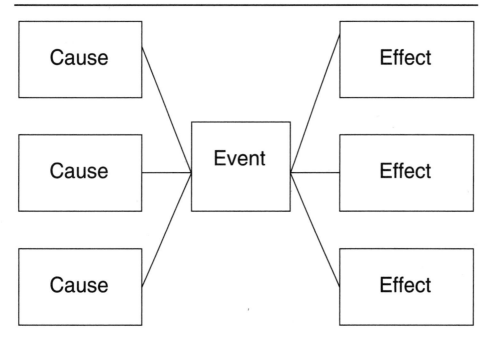

#7: SEEING SIMILARITIES AND DIFFERENCES

Discerning similarities and differences among concepts can increase student understanding. Students' prior knowledge can be compared and contrasted with new concepts. Graphic forms such as Venn diagrams and visual analogies can effectively bridge prior and new knowledge. Teachers can present, or ask students to identify, similarities and differences using examples such as the two shown in Figures 1.7A and B.

Figure 1.7A A Visual Analogy of Similarities

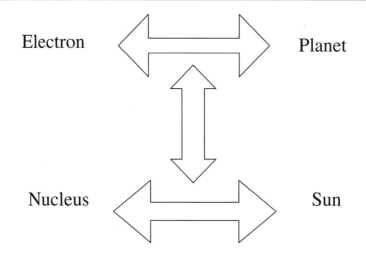

Figure 1.7B A Venn Diagram of Similarities and Differences

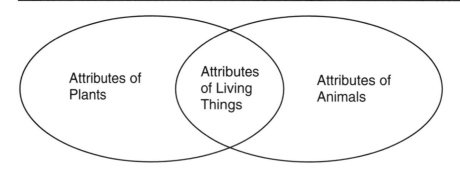

#8: THE WHOLE AND ITS PARTS

Students benefit from being introduced to the big-picture concept of what they are studying (see Figure 1.8). Once this is made explicit, they can identify the major and minor components of the overall concept they already know and fill in the rest as they proceed. Questions teachers can pose to elicit prior knowledge include: What is the concept we are considering? What are its main parts? What are some of its subparts?

Figure 1.8 A Divided Whole

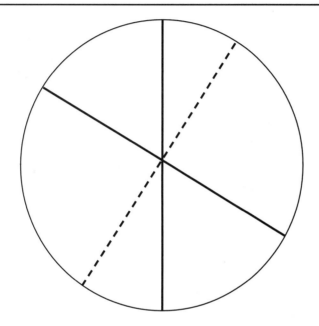

#9: SPEAKING CATEGORICALLY

Building on graphic forms, this activity asks students to brainstorm using their prior knowledge about a concept and then work from parts to major categories (see Figure 1.9). To begin, put the topic you are about to teach in the middle of a blackboard or on a chart. Ask students for associations and log their responses nonsequentially around the concept. For example, in Step A, students brainstormed modes of transportation. Next, in Step B, they identified categories that emerged from their previous associations. In Step C, the categories were specified.

Figure 1.9 Brainstorming Diagrams

Step A

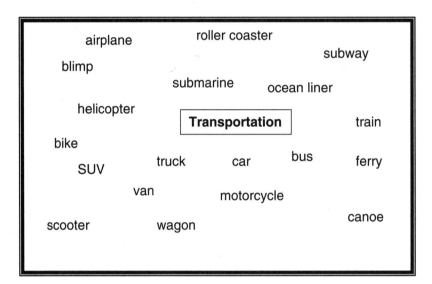

Step B

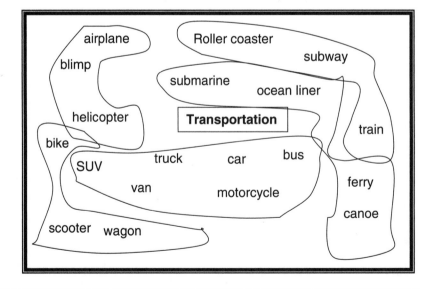

Step C

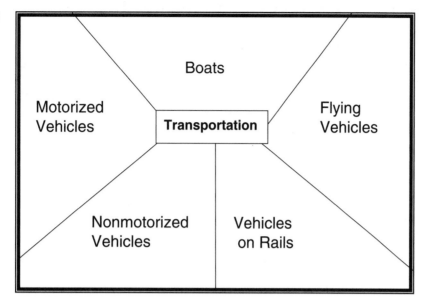

#10: COMMONLY SHARED PRIOR EXPERIENCES

Another approach to activating background knowledge is providing experiences that evoke it. A classroom experience that provides a common reference point for all students can precede a unit. See if one or more of the following might be appropriate for your classroom:

- Give a demonstration.
  Example 1: If you are introducing a new writing convention, first read a letter that you have written containing a few mistakes. As in a *Daily Oral Language* activity, have the students try to identify the errors.
  Example 2: If you are teaching about an historical event or geographical feature, begin by showing students a timeline, illustration, map, or globe.

- Explain the new topic from your experience.
  Example 1: In literature, suggest how the story relates to something in another book or in your own life.
  Example 2: In math, explain how you use the skills being taught in everyday life. Discuss with the class how they use the skills outside of school.

- Read a brief news article that addresses the content.
  Example 1: Newspaper articles can illustrate parts of speech, stylistic elements, conventions, purposes, and categories such as editorial opinions, sports events, question and answer columns, or political cartoons.
  Example 2: For social studies, read a news article and compare it to an historical event. For example, show how a current conflict resembles a past war or a current leader compares with a previous one; or point out differences and similarities in past and current social fashions.

- Show a video clip, poster, or timeline.
  Examples: For a math lesson, show a homemade video of people actually using math skills. For a health lesson, show a poster or overhead transparency depicting the concept you intend to teach.

- Tell a story.
  Examples: Use a picture book, personal experience, or fairytale as a metaphor for something you plan to teach. For example, Aesop's (n.d.) *Fables* illustrate moral and mathematical issues. True stories about real people in the past can introduce historical periods.

- Preteach vocabulary.

#11: CHARTING A COLORFUL COURSE

This process elicits and builds background knowledge simultaneously. To begin, think of five questions about the content students will learn. Write one question each on five large sheets of blank newsprint paper. Hang the sheets on the walls at various points around the classroom. Divide students into groups of four to six and give one person in each group a marker that differs in color from those given to the other groups. Assign each group to begin at one of the five charts. While at their charts, the groups should brainstorm responses to the posted questions; the reporters log the groups' responses. After two minutes, signal the groups to move to the right to the next chart. Once again, they brainstorm responses to the questions and log them on the second chart. The process continues until each group has brainstormed responses to all five questions. The groups should return to their original charts, review the content, form clusters of related ideas in categories they choose, and eliminate repeated concepts. The groups can also be asked to check for accuracy, identify questions, and summarize what their classmates know. They should then share key ideas from their charts with the rest of the class.

#12: ASKING THE RIGHT QUESTIONS

Prior knowledge can be easily activated through any number of questions and the resulting discussions. Some sample questions follow.

- What have we studied before that is similar to this?
- What are first-hand experiences we have had with this concept?
- Who knows something about this concept?
- What are other words we could use for . . . ?
- Who has questions about this topic?
- What does this remind you of?
- What do you remember about this?
- What do you associate with this topic?
- What made you think of such associations?
- Where or when would this be useful?
- Using what we have already learned, can someone walk us through solving this problem step by step?
- How can we extend this to . . . ?
- Where outside of the classroom might you be able to use this?

#13: GUIDED ANTICIPATION

Anticipation guides orient students to a lesson's content. Whether in the form of checklists, true or false quizzes, or worksheets, guides can build on students' prior knowledge, explain the purpose of a lesson, and spark interest and curiosity in learning. Figure 1.10 supplies a sample of an anticipation guide for a reading selection.

Figure 1.10 Anticipation Guide

Pre-Reading Guide

Title of text to be read:

Main topic:

What I think I already know about this topic:

What I think I'll read:

A question I have is:

#14: THINKING OUT LOUD

When teachers explain their thought processes, students can learn how to tap their background knowledge and approach problem-solving tasks. Teacher mentoring of out-loud thinking enables students to identify and replicate strategies that will improve their cognitive processes (Davey, 1983). Thinking aloud can be used in any number of ways: solving math problems or beginning a writing project, for instance. Below are six steps for modeling thinking aloud in the classroom:

- Step 1: Identify a skill or concept you want students to learn.
- Step 2: Explain to students that you are going to think out loud about how you would approach the task. Students should not interrupt you but rather observe the strategies you explain.
- Step 3: Think aloud through the task by asking questions about
  – Your attitude toward the assignment
  – What you think you know about the topic
  – First steps to take
  – Possible alternatives
  – Self-corrections
  – How you will proceed with the task
- Step 4: Afterward, ask students to tell you the processes they heard and observed you utilize. Write these on an overhead or blackboard, and analyze whether similar processes might be beneficial when students are engaged in a learning task. Also inquire about additional strategies students can suggest.
- Step 5: Assign a task and ask a student volunteer to model out-loud thinking in front of the class *or* organize small groups with one or two think-out-loud volunteers in each.
- Step 6: Coach students in their thinking as they work through similar tasks.

#15: USING PRIOR KNOWLEDGE BEFORE, DURING, AND AFTER A LESSON

Linking students' prior knowledge with the new content at hand—before, during, and after a lesson—can increase comprehension.

Before a Lesson

Activate prior knowledge by brainstorming or summarizing previous learning.

During a Lesson

Help students identify key points, check their predictions, and draw analogies between the new content and what they have learned previously from life and from school. Ask if it is appropriate to modify any of their ideas.

After a Lesson

Ask students to extend what they learned to their lives and schooling. Discuss whether the lesson changed their preexisting ideas and how they envision applying the new information.

SUGGESTED READINGS
FOR FURTHER INFORMATION

Bransford, J. D., Brown, A. L., & Cocking, R. R. (Eds.). (1999). *How People Learn: Brain, Mind, Experience, and School.* Washington, DC: National Academy Press.

This book synthesizes research on the science of learning. Its expansive scope includes how learning occurs, the differences between expert and novice performance, children as learners, the development of learning environments, and new technologies. The editors also address how transfer takes place and the critical role of existing knowledge in conceptual change.

Gardner, H. (1991). *The Unschooled Mind: How Children Think and How Schools Should Teach.* New York: Basic Books.

In this book, Gardner explores why children fail to master what schools teach. He hypothesizes that children construct durable "workaday" notions about life, objects, self, and others by the age of 5 or 6. Because schools typically teach in rote, mimetic ways, students' self-constructed theories endure, preventing in-depth disciplinary understanding from being realized. To dislodge student misconceptions, Gardner suggests ways schools might teach to achieve meaningful understanding.

Roschelle, J. (1997). *Learning in Interactive Environments: Prior Knowledge and New Experience.* Retrieved from Institute for Inquiry, December 27, 2000: netra. exploratorium.edu/IFI/resources/museumeducation/priorknowledge.html

This article reviews the application of prior knowledge to mathematics, science, and museum education. Roschelle addresses a central debate about the concept: its positive and negative roles in construction of knowledge. Readers interested in the theoretical perspectives of this concept will likely enjoy Roschelle's descriptions of Piaget, Dewey, Vygotsky, and other theorists who have contributed to our understanding of prior knowledge.

REFERENCES

Aesop. (n.d.). Fables. Retrieved August 2, 2002, from aesopfables.com

Ball, D. (1993). With an eye on the mathematical horizon: Dilemmas of teaching elementary school mathematics. *Elementary School Journal, 93,* 373-397.

Carey, S., & Gelman, R. (Eds.). (1991). *The epigenesis of mind: Essays on biology and cognition.* Hillsdale, NJ: Lawrence Erlbaum.

Carpenter, T., & Fennema, E. (1992). Cognitively guided instruction: Building on the knowledge of students and teachers. *International Journal of Educational Research, 17,* 457-470.

Carpenter, T., Fennema, E., & Franke, M. (1996). Cognitively guided instruction: A knowledge base for reform in primary mathematics instruction. *Elementary School Journal, 97*(1), 3-20.

Clement, J., Brown, D., & Zeitsman, A. (1989). Not all preconceptions are misconceptions: Finding anchoring conceptions for grounding instruction on students' intuitions. *International Journal of Science Education, 11*(5), 554-565.

Christen, W. L., & Murphy, T. J. (1991). Increasing comprehension by activating prior knowledge. ERIC Digest #61. Bloomington, IN: ERIC Clearinghouse on Reading, English, and Communication. (ERIC Document Reproduction Service No. ED 328 885)

Davey, B. (1983, October). Thinking aloud: Modeling the cognitive processes of reading comprehension. *Journal of Reading,* pp. 44-47.

Gardner, H. (1991). *The unschooled mind: How children think and how schools should teach.* New York: Basic Books.

Graves, M., & Cook, C. (1980). Effects of previewing difficult short stories for high school students. *Research on Reading in Secondary Schools, 6,* 38-54, 256-80.

Hayes, D., & Tierney, R. (1982). Developing readers' knowledge through analogy. *Reading Research Quarterly, 17*(2), 256-80.

Lambert, M. (1986). Knowing, doing, and teaching multiplication. *Cognition and Instruction, 3,* 305-342.

Marzano, R. (1998). *A theory-based meta-anlaysis of research on instruction.* Aurora, CO: Mid-Continent Regional Educational Laboratory.

Minstrell, J. (1989). Teaching science for understanding. In L. B. Resnick & L. Klopfer (Eds.), *Towards the thinking curriculum* (pp. 129-149). Alexandria, VA: Association for Supervision and Curriculum Development.

Ogle, D. S. (1986). K-W-L group instructional strategy. In A. Palinscar, D. S. Ogle, B. F. Jones, & E. G. Carr (Eds.), *Teaching reading as thinking: Teleconference resource guide* (pp. 11-17). Alexandria, VA: Association for Supervision and Curriculum Development.

Piaget, J. (1968). *Judgment and reasoning in the child* (M. Warden, Trans.). Totowa, NJ: Littlefield & Adams.

Roschelle, J. (1997). *Learning interactive environments: Prior knowledge and new experience.* Retrieved August 3, 2002, from the Institute for Inquiry, netra.exploratorium. edu/IFI/resources/museumeducation/priorknowledge.html

Stevens, K. (1982, January). Can we improve reading by teaching background information? *Journal of Reading, 25,* 326-29.

Vacca, R. (1981). *Content area reading.* Baston: Little, Brown.

2

Active Learning

An Essential Classroom Ingredient

If you attempt to recall a particularly memorable learning experience, it likely was one that engaged you in multisensory ways. You probably discovered an insight that was relevant and meaningful then and now. Such experiences reveal that learning is not a spectator sport. As Glasser (1990) found in a study of high schools, students do not mind working hard. What they do mind is being bored by rote, repetitive tasks that avoid engaging their minds and bodies.

It comes as no surprise that representatives from several K-12 disciplines such as reading, art, social studies, and writing, share similar opinions about best practices for instruction. Curriculum reports from the National Council of Teachers of Mathematics, the Center for the Study of Reading, the National Writing Project, the National Council for Social Studies, the American Association for the Advancement of Science, the National Council of Teachers of English, and the National Association for the Education of Young Children, all recommend instructional practices that include experiential, active, hands-on learning (Zemelman, Daniels, & Hyde, 1998).

Noneducators concur with these recommendations. For example, Meltzoff (D'Arcangelo, 2000), a developmental psychologist, asserts that, "Stimulating, varied input is important for development, starting from the earliest ages all the way through college and into adulthood . . . activity in learning is very important. Children don't learn well from having information passively presented to them" (p. 11). Similarly, neuroscientist Diamond and Hopson (1998) defines enrichment as "pursuing activities that are fun, interesting, even exciting to a child and that provide challenge and stimulation while requiring active involvement" (p. 283). Learning depends on the input of rich sensory data, and we might even say that it is activity dependent. We learn through challenges, sensory stimulation, and interactivity.

WHY IS ACTIVE LEARNING IMPORTANT?

Regardless of the similarity in neurological architecture, each person is wired to perceive, process, and demonstrate learning in highly individualized ways. Not all minds work in the same way when presented with the same teacher and textbooks. Students succeed academically but not necessarily in the same way as their peers. By varying our pedagogical approaches, we can meet more of our students' needs more of the time. Variety banishes boredom, engages attention, enlivens learning, and helps embed information in memory.

Perhaps our parents, or those of us who are baby boomers, succeeded with a passive approach to learning, but the increasing diversity of K-12 students living in a technologically drenched society necessitates the use of highly interactive classroom practices. Students come to us from a variety of cultures and life experiences, reveal different ability levels, and are immersed in a multimedia world. No single teaching approach will adequately respond to everyone in today's classrooms. Most teachers infuse variety into their instruction to motivate and inspire learning, but we need to ensure that our multifaceted approaches are meaningful, appropriate, and well conceived. Fortunately, there are principles from cognitive-sciences research that indicate ways to mindfully enhance classroom practice.

The new science of learning reveals that both facts and "big picture" ideas (Bransford, Brown, & Cocking, 1999) must be addressed in our units. Students need opportunities to understand the purpose behind why and what they are learning to avoid getting lost in a part-to-whole method. Meaningful patterns of information must be shared along with individual facts and skills.

We have also realized that while active learning is a necessity across the curriculum, the subject areas approach this principle differently (Cawelti, 1999; Darling-Hammond, 1996; Shulman, 1987). Active teaching across disciplines often varies because knowledge in each is organized differently and based on different ways of knowing. For example, in language arts, students should engage in storytelling, composing, and reading literature and nonfiction texts, and use diverse speaking and listening skills appropriate for multiple audiences. In mathematics, manipulatives and real-world projects can teach the essentials of sorting, counting, and perceiving patterns of number and shape. In science, students can pursue answers to open-ended questions and justify their responses. They can conduct experiments and take field trips to fine-tune their observation and investigation skills. In social studies, students can conduct opinion surveys, role play famous events, conduct their classrooms as democracies, and hold political debates.

WHAT DOES THE RESEARCH SHOW ABOUT ACTIVE LEARNING?

In an extensive review of research on effective educational practices, Marzano, Pickering, and Pollack (2001) identified practices that result in increased student achievement. Knowledge is stored linguistically and, importantly, nonlinguistically. This means that when teachers and students use language along with images, and movement to learn, understanding and achievement increase. Likewise, working collaboratively in groups, and setting and reflecting on goals improve achievement in all disciplines and at all grade levels. Much of this chapter addresses multimodal forms of learning allowing students to tap their linguistic and nonlinguistic cognitive resources.

Specifically, the instructional strategies in this chapter fall into three broad categories: (a) techniques that address whole-to-part and part-to-whole instruction, (b) disciplinary-specific approaches, and (c) generic, multidisciplinary approaches based on Gardner's (1983) multiple intelligences (which some consider closely aligned to arts-based teaching). Studies of these three approaches reveal the role they can play in enhancing classroom success.

The first set of mindful strategies, those balancing whole-to-part instruction, underscores the need of many students to learn facts and their underlying principles. Learning must be guided by generalized principles to be widely transferred and applied (Bransford, Brown, & Cocking, 1999). Many times students are faced with bits and pieces of tasks that lack apparent meaning, and they achieve accordingly (Klausmeier, 1985). Cultural issues also come into play. Several studies have demonstrated that many non-Euro American students underachieve because their "holistic" or "field-dependent" versus "analytic" or "field-independent" cognitive orientation is overlooked in schools (Howard, 1987; Kuykendall, 1991; Ramirez & Casteneda, 1974; Shade, 1989; Tharp, 1994; Witkin, Goodenough, Moore, & Cox, 1977). Holistic or field-dependent learners need to understand the big picture and learn by moving from the general to the specific, while analytic or field-independent thinkers are comfortable learning from the parts to the whole. As a result, classroom instruction needs to address both the forest and the trees.

Another set of strategies in this chapter is specific to various disciplines. In addition to general pedagogical and content knowledge, student achievement increases when their teachers know how to approach the teaching of individual disciplines (Bransford, Brown, & Cocking, 1999; Cawelti, 1999; Darling-Hammond, 1996). Recently developed standards in the various disciplines necessitate that content knowledge be taught in depth. This does not negate the fact that many teachers are integrating curriculum to help students perceive relationships among concepts. In fact, most elementary teachers have natural settings for such integration, and many secondary teachers are shifting to interdisciplinary block formats. At the same time, for the purposes of this book, research- and discipline-based practices are described.

The third set of strategies is based on cognitive scientist Gardner's (1983, 1995) theory of multiple intelligences (MI). Though widely popular in educational circles for nearly 20 years, his theories have been the subject of little research and, until recently, were conducted on the effectiveness of long-held theories of instruction and student achievement. As you likely know, MI theory hypothesizes that human competence consists of at least eight forms of intelligence: linguistic, mathematical, musical, kinesthetic, visual, interpersonal, intrapersonal, and naturalistic. Many teachers transformed the eight intelligences into pedagogical techniques, theorizing that they would enliven learning and engage students' strengths. What's been learned? A study conducted by the American Institutes for Research and reported by the American Association of School Administrators (2001) showed that schools adopting an MI model called "Different Ways of Knowing" achieved strong student gains in the basic skills. The strongest gains were in language arts, math, and social studies.

In a case study of six schools using MI-based instruction, Campbell and Campbell (1999) found that basic-skills achievement increased as measured by state assessments and standardized scores. Similarly, the award-winning Eugene Field Accelerated School in Jefferson City, Missouri, realized strong gains in Missouri Mastery and Achievement Test scores which were "attributed to the staff's focus on and implementation of the multiple intelligences in every classroom" (Missouri Department of Elementary and Secondary Education, 1998). Fiske's (1999) research, which is similar to MI theory, shows that student performance increased with arts-enriched curriculum. (A caveat is in order—I am not suggesting that the arts be taught solely to enhance other subjects. My stance is that they deserve to be taught as separate disciplines and used secondarily as instructional methods.)

ACTIVE LEARNING IN THE CLASSROOM

The rationales for teachers to diversify their instruction are plentiful. The challenges to do so are enormous—and exciting. Active learning engages students, enriches the curriculum, and nurtures meaning and relevance for everyone. In the pages that follow are strategies that fall into three categories: (a) whole-to-part instruction or, as we call it, getting the big idea; (b) MI-based teaching, and (c) discipline-specific instruction. It should be noted that many of the MI activities are useful for the disciplines of language arts, mathematics, science, and the arts. The discipline-specific strategies address reading, social studies, mathematics, and health.

#16: GETTING THE BIG IDEA WITH CUE CARDS

Students can be introduced to big ideas—the principles, concepts, or theories that serve as the adhesive glue for facts at the outset of a lesson or unit. Figures 2.1A and 2.1B present two examples of verbal road maps to enhance student understanding. The first is a teacher's cue card that offers questions to guide student thinking. The second road map helps students distinguish main ideas from supporting details in a reading selection.

Figure 2.1A Cue Card for Teacher

Teacher's Cue Card
Step 1: Review previous learning. What did we learn yesterday? How could that information be used at home or at school?
Step 2: Personalize learning. What did this information make you think about? What would happen if you used this information? Why?
Step 3: Define key concept. How would you define ___?
Step 4: Clarify next step. What we will study next is ____. The reason why is ___. Where do you think we will go from here?

Figure 2.1B Cue Card for Student

Student Directions for Finding the Big Idea
Step 1: Brainstorm any ideas that come to mind about the reading selection before reading it.
Step 2: Read the selection taking at least two pages of detailed notes.
Step 3: Summarize your notes into one page.
Step 4: Summarize your notes into a half page.
Step 5: Summarize your notes into a quarter page.
Step 6: Summarize your notes into one big idea.
Step 7: Compare your big idea with your brainstorming. What similarities and differences exist?
Step 8: Step back—what is the big picture?

#17: GETTING THE BIG IDEA: VISUAL REPORT WRITING

Graphic organizers can effectively portray a complete product while showing how its parts contribute to the whole. The sample organizer in Figure 2.2 gives a visual outline for writing a report.

Figure 2.2 Visual Organizer for Report or Essay

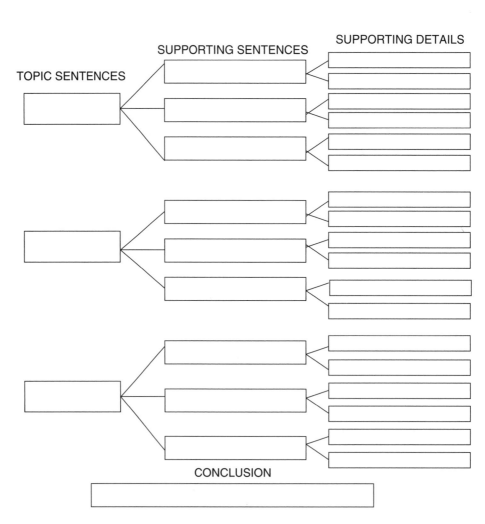

SOURCE: From Linda Campbell, Bruce Campbell, & Dee Dickinson. *Teaching and Learning Through Multiple Intelligences,* 2nd Edition (p. 102). Published by Allyn & Bacon, Boston, MA. Copyright © 1999 by Pearson Education. Adapted by permission of the publisher.

#18: VISUAL STORY MAPPING

The organizer in Figure 2.3 helps students identify the parts of a story or novel and in so doing enhances comprehension.

Figure 2.3 Story Map

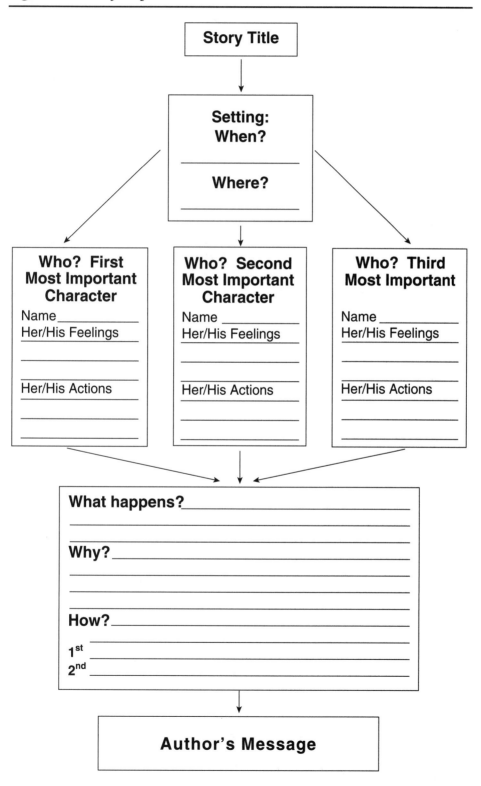

SOURCE: Adapted from I. Beck & M. McKeown (1981).

#19: VISUALLY TRACKING A CLASSROOM UNIT

Some teachers provide students with visual overviews of entire units (see Figure 2.4). They do this by creating a bulletin board, a notebook, or chart showing the unit's components. As each item is covered, students log their learning onto the classroom tracking sheet or onto charts in their notebooks.

Figure 2.4 Overview Organizer

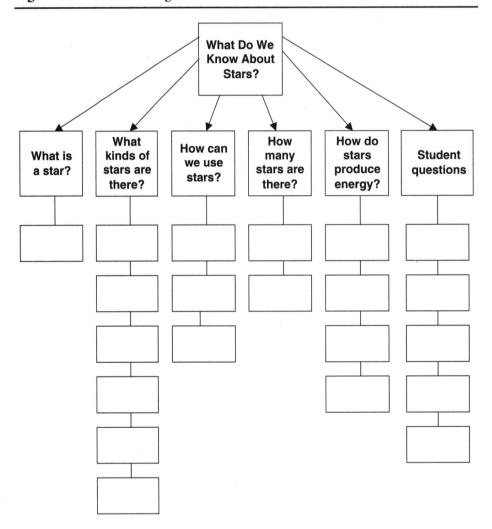

#20: LINGUISTICALLY INTELLIGENT LEARNING

Gardner's (1983) theory of MI has spawned numerous instructional adaptations. Linguistic intelligence incorporates the broad areas of listening, speaking, writing, and reading. Diverse instructional strategies to engage a spectrum of human competencies in learning are listed here and in other strategies in this chapter. These are adapted from Campbell, Campbell, and Dickinson (1999, p. 265):

Linguistically Intelligent Learning Strategies

- Memorize and tell a story about . . .
- Participate in a debate about . . .
- Compose a poem about . . .
- Prepare and give a presentation on . . .
- Read a children's book to a child about . . .
- Make up slogans for . . .
- Facilitate a classroom discussion about . . .
- Create a radio talk show about . . .
- Write a book report for . . .
- Create a word puzzle of . . .
- Interview a knowledgeable person about . . .
- Write an editorial about . . .
- Use a word processing program to . . .
- Create a dictionary of . . .
- Listen to a lecture and identify key ideas. . . .
- Summarize a news article. . . .

#21: GUIDED LISTENING

Students frequently spend classroom time listening to learn. Teaching explicit listening techniques can improve this fundamental linguistic skill. Figure 2.5 focuses student attention on key points while encouraging them to think critically about what they are hearing. The guide can be used for class lectures, guest speakers, and student presentations.

Figure 2.5 Focusing Tool

Student name:_____

Speaker's name: _____

Title or purpose of talk: _____

_____

Main idea: _____

_____

    Supporting details: _____

_____

_____

Main idea: _____

_____

    Supporting details: _____

_____

_____

Fill in as appropriate:

Vocabulary:	Definitions:
Problem:	Suggested Solution:
Procedure:	Steps:
Opinion:	Rationale:

One sentence summary:_____

_____

#22: MATHEMATICALLY INTELLIGENT LEARNING

The list below features strategies to promote mathematical thinking across the curriculum and is adapted from Campbell and colleagues (1999, p. 265). This broad area of human intellectual competence includes the ability to think logically, mathematically, and scientifically.

Mathematically Intelligent Learning Strategies

- Identify the patterns in . . .
- Predict the logical outcomes of . . .
- Develop a graph or chart of . . .
- Translate . . . into a formula that . . .
- Create a timeline of . . .
- Systematically investigate . . .
- Sequence the events in . . .
- Write a story problem for . . .
- Develop a system to record data for . . .
- Analyze and draw a conclusion for . . .
- Create a budget for . . .
- Use a calculator to . . .
- Solve an open-ended problem about . . .
- Put . . . into an outline format that. . .

#23: REAL-LIFE MATHEMATICAL PROBLEM SOLVING

Contrary to the math problems found in textbooks, many of those found in real-life situations are open-ended in nature. Identifying and solving such problems reinforces mathematical skills and shows the relevance of math in everyday life. A nine-step process for open-ended problem solving follows. Sample problems might include identifying the amount of waste an average person generates in a day, week, or month—or determining the average number of grams of fat in common snacks.

- Step 1: Identify a math problem.
- Step 2: Identify the variables to be considered in problem solving.
- Step 3: Specify the types of data that must be gathered.
- Step 4: Systematically collect data.
- Step 5: Organize and analyze the data.
- Step 6: Identify patterns in the data. Note, too, any contradictory data.
- Step 7: Draw tentative conclusions.
- Step 8: Verify conclusions by asking others to review the data.
- Step 9: Make recommendations or explain conclusions.

#24: KINESTHETICALLY INTELLIGENT LEARNING

Kinesthetic intelligence refers to an ability to unite the body and mind in physical performance. Learning by doing is often unforgettable since the mind remembers what the body experiences. Strategies for using kinesthetic learning across the curriculum follow. They are adapted from Campbell and colleagues (1999, p. 265).

Kinesthetically Intelligent Learning Strategies

- Improvise or simulate . . .
- Make a board or floor game of . . .
- Construct a model of . . .
- Participate in a scavenger hunt to gather data about . . .
- Use manipulatives to . . .
- Develop a product for . . .
- Create and play a game about . . .
- Improve physical skills for . . .
- Be mentored by . . . for . . .
- Go on a field trip to . . .
- Enact . . . through mime.
- Create a kinesthetic flow chart of . . .

#25: JIGSAW CARDS AND PUZZLES

Jigsaw cards and puzzles are simple games students make from card stock to reinforce learning. Sets of cards can be stored for future use. Samples are shown in Figure 2.6.

Figure 2.6 Jigsaws

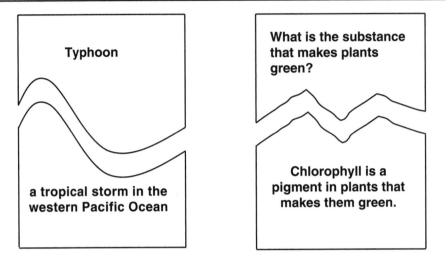

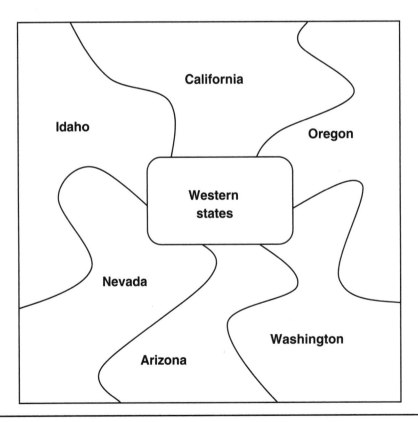

SOURCE: From Rita and Kenneth Dunn, *Teaching Students Through Their Individual Learning Styles: A Practical Approach.* Published by Allyn & Bacon, Boston, MA. Copyright © 1978 by Pearson Education. Adapted by permission of the publisher.

#26: VISUALLY INTELLIGENT LEARNING

Visual intelligence enables us to perceive internal and external imagery. It involves the ability to recreate, transform, or modify images, to move ourselves and objects through space, and to produce or decode graphic images. A list of visual techniques to enliven learning follows. They are adapted from Campbell and colleagues (1999, p. 265).

Visually Intelligent Learning Strategies

- Use the overhead projector to . . .
- Make a collage for . . .
- Color code the steps of . . .
- Design a poster or bulletin board of . . .
- Illustrate or draw . . .
- Use graphic organizers to . . .
- Create an advertisement for . . .
- Use mental imagery to imagine . . .
- Use multimedia to . . .
- Vary the color and size of print to . . .
- Make a scroll for . . .
- Create a photographic essay of . . .

#27: MAKING A GEOGRAPHY GAME

One example of visual intelligence applied to classroom learning is to make and play board games. This strategy involves a simple classroom-made geography game. Additional game boards could be made of the solar system, a DNA molecule, or a town or city. Once made, games can be stored for future use.

1. Identify the purpose of the game; for example, to teach about Africa's geography.

2. Design the game board specifying whether it will have an original or commercially adapted format. The example in Figure 2.7 uses a simple path.

3. Decide how the game will be won.

4. Draw a rough draft on a piece of paper.

5. Decide how players will move through the game; for instance, with dice, cards, or spinners.

6. Transfer the rough draft to card stock or cardboard, complete the game board, and play.

Figure 2.7 Geography Game

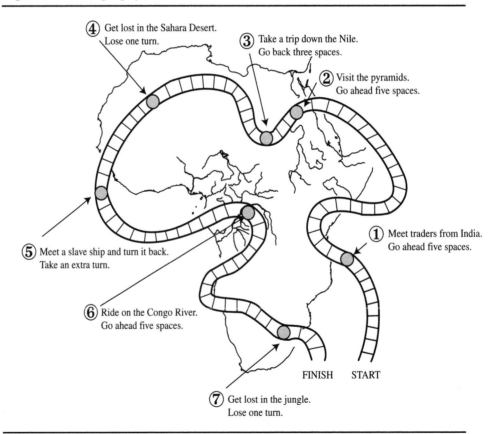

SOURCE: From Linda Campbell, Bruce Campbell, and Dee Dickinson. *Teaching and Learning Through Multiple Intelligences.* 2nd Edition (p. 116). Published by Allyn & Bacon, Boston, MA. Copyright © 1999 by Pearson Education. Adapted by permission of the publisher.

#28: MUSICALLY INTELLIGENT LEARNING

Musical intelligence is evident in those individuals who possess a sensitivity to pitch, melody, rhythm, and tone. In the classroom, music can dramatically enhance learning and social dynamics. Several strategies adapted from Campbell and colleagues (1999, p. 265) are provided for using music across the curriculum.

Musically Intelligent Learning Strategies

- Use musical accompaniment to present . . .
- Write song lyrics for . . .
- Sing a song about . . .
- Find and play a song that represents . . .
- Add sound effects to . . .
- Play music to create an ambiance of . . .
- Make up a chant or jingle about . . .
- Present a short musical on . . .
- Use environmental sounds to . . .
- Conduct a rhythmic choral reading to . . .
- Memorize concepts musically. . . .
- Write new lyrics to a well-known song to memorize. . . .
- Explore aspects of another culture through music. . . .

#29: MUSICALLY INSPIRED CREATIVE WRITING

A combination of musical and linguistic intelligence can lead not only to song writing but also to creative writing. This strategy shows how to use music to jumpstart creative writing efforts.

- Step 1: Select four musical selections to play in class.
- Step 2: Tell students that you will play two or three minutes of the first selection, and that they should pretend to be film producers who must create a storyline for the musical score.
- Step 3: Play the music and discuss the movie ideas.
- Step 4: Next, tell students you will play a second brief piece, and after that, they should let the music suggest a setting and character for a story. After they listen, ask students to write their story ideas.
- Step 5: Play a sharply contrasting third selection and tell students to let the music suggest a second character and some type of problem or conflict. Ask them to continue writing their stories.
- Step 6: Play the fourth selection and suggest that students imagine an interaction among the characters and write about it.
- Step 7: Play the second selection once again and tell students to imagine the problem or conflict being resolved and to write an ending for their stories.

SOURCE: From Linda Campbell, Bruce Campbell, and Dee Dickinson. *Teaching and Learning Through Multiple Intelligences.* 2nd Edition (p. 151). Published by Allyn & Bacon, Boston, MA. Copyright © 1999 by Pearson Education. Adapted by permission of the publisher.

#30: INTERPERSONALLY INTELLIGENT LEARNING

Interpersonal intelligence is a cluster of complex skills that enables us to understand and communicate with others; to perceive differences in moods, temperaments, and motivations; to forge and sustain relationships; and to assume various roles in groups. The following list suggests ways to engage and strengthen social skills in the classroom. They are adapted from Campbell and colleagues (1999, p. 265).

Interpersonally Intelligent Learning Strategies

- Work with a partner, a small group, or a large group to . . .
- Perform a class job: . . .
- Role play diverse perspectives about . . .
- Assume a role in a group to . . .
- Teach someone else about . . .
- Plan rules for participation in . . .
- Give and receive feedback on . . .
- Do a service project for . . .
- Use a conflict resolution technique to . . .
- Identify a social skill to refine . . .
- Use one of your strengths in . . .
- Cooperate with others to . . .
- Assume a leadership role to . . .
- Identify a stereotype in . . .
- Consider the social consequences of . . .
- Identify a cultural value that differs from your own. . . .

#31: MASS MEDIA'S MESSAGES

One significant communicator of interpersonal messages is the mass media. This activity asks students to critically consider the ways in which social roles and norms are portrayed by mass media.

Age, Race, Ethnicity, and Physical Characteristics

- Who is represented?
- Who is left out?
- What is the main message?

Children

- What differences exist in roles for male and female children?
- How are children depicted?
- Who nurtures the children?

Masculine and Feminine Characteristics

- How do the portrayals of men and women differ?
- What kind of personalities do men and women have?

Careers

- What kinds of careers are portrayed?
- List the male and female jobs or careers.

Relationships

- What kinds of relationships do the genders have?
- Is one gender more dominant than the other?
- Are the relationships realistic or fairytale-like?

Sex and Violence

- Is sex used to sell a product or a show?
- How is violence portrayed?
- What is more dominant—the product, the story, violence, or sex?

#32: INTRAPERSONALLY INTELLIGENT LEARNING

Intrapersonal intelligence consists of the ability to construct an accurate perception of oneself and to use such knowledge in planning and directing one's life. The intrapersonal strategies here encourage students to engage their interests and feelings in learning. They are adapted from Campbell and colleagues (1999, p. 265).

Intrapersonally Intelligent Learning Strategies

- Identify what interests you about . . .
- Explain how . . . is relevant to you. . . .
- Set a goal to . . .
- Write a journal entry about . . .
- Describe what motivates you. . . .
- Self-assess your work for . . .
- Explain your feelings about . . .
- Describe an important value . . .
- Identify someone you admire . . .
- Share an insight you had about . . .
- Create a personal motto for . . .
- Describe a strong interest. . . .
- Explain how you learn best. . . .
- Identify short and long-term goals. . . .

#33: TAPPING STUDENT INTERESTS WITH PROJECTS

Students enjoy tapping their intrapersonal intelligence to take charge of their learning, and autonomy can be nurtured through project-based learning. At first, students may need assistance with the eight steps of completing projects but their self-directed learning skills will increase over time.

Eight Steps for Project-Based Learning

1. State your goal.

   I want to understand how visual illusions work.

2. Put your goal into one or more questions.

   What are visual illusions? How do they fool our eyes?

3. List at least three sources of information you will use.

   Eye doctors or university professors, library books on visual illusions, prints of M. C. Escher's work, and the art teacher

4. Describe the steps you will take to achieve your goal.

   Ask the librarian to find books on visual illusions.

   Look up visual illusions in the encyclopedia.

   Look for visual illusions on the Internet.

   Talk to the art teacher and other experts about visual illusions.

   Look at Escher's work.

5. List at least five main concepts or ideas you want to research.

   What are visual illusions?

   How is the human eye (or brain) tricked?

   How are visual illusions made?

   Who are some artists who have made visual illusions?

   Can I learn to make some visual illusions?

6. List at least three methods you will use to present your project.

   Explain what visual illusions are.

   Make a diagram of how the human eye works.

   Make posters with famous visual illusions.

   Make visual illusions of my own.

Hand out a sheet of visual illusions for class members to keep.

Have the class try to make some.

7. Organize the project into a timeline.

   Week 1: Read sources of information.

   Week 1: Interview adults.

   Week 1: Look at a variety of visual illusions.

   Week 2: Try to make visual illusions.

   Week 2: Make diagram of eye and brain.

   Week 2: Make handouts for class.

   Week 3: Practice presentation.

   Week 3: Present to class.

8. Decide how you will evaluate your project.

   Practice it in front of my parents and get their feedback.

   Practice in front of Matt and Jamal and get their feedback.

   Ask class for feedback on my presentation and visuals.

   Fill out self-evaluation form.

   Read teacher's evaluation.

   Analyze videotape.

SOURCE: From Bruce Campbell. *The Multiple Intelligences Handbook: Lesson Plans and More* (pp. 140-141). Published by Campbell & Associates. Copyright © 1994. Reprinted by permission of the publisher.

#34: NATURALISTICALLY INTELLIGENT LEARNING

Naturalistic intelligence consists of observing patterns in nature, identifying and classifying objects, and understanding natural and human-made systems. The list of strategies, adapted from Campbell and colleagues (1999, p. 265), suggests diverse ways to activate the thinking of a naturalist across the curriculum.

Naturalistically Intelligent Learning Strategies

- Gather and classify data.
- Maintain an observation notebook.
- Compare natural phenomena to . . .
- Create categories for . . .
- Compare an animal to . . .
- Contrast a plant with . . .
- Attend a field trip to observe . . .
- Create a taxonomy for . . .
- Describe relationships among . . .
- Identify the patterns in . . .
- Describe the characteristics of . . .
- Make a classification chart of . . .

#35: IT'S CLASSIFIED!

The naturalist's ability to classify items is engaged by the strategy below. The relationships among subordinate ideas become evident at a glance. Figure 2.8 shows a blank classification tree followed by a sample of a completed form on the geography of the earth.

Figure 2.8 Classification Tree

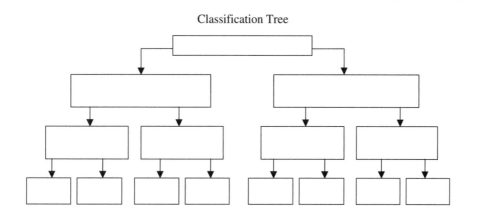

Classification trees are not only helpful for recording and reading taxonomies, they can also be applied to other data, as the following geography classification tree demonstrates.

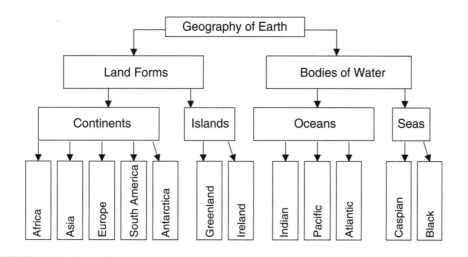

#36 VOCABULARY WORD SAVVY

Many teachers assign spelling or vocabulary words each week or at the outset of a unit. Sometimes students can more easily remember a word when they perceive its broader context. The examples in Figures 2.9A and 2.9B ask students to define words and more.

Figure 2.9A   Word Definition Diagram

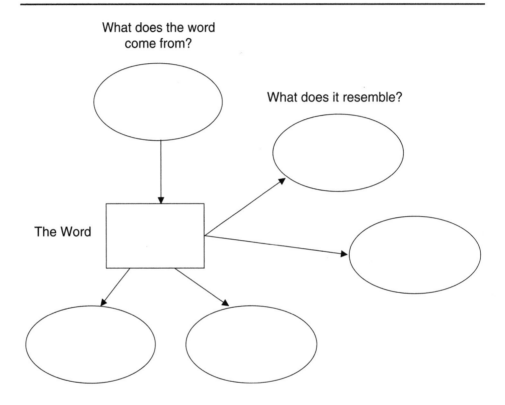

Figure 2.9B   Word Star

Similar to Word Maps, Word Stars can be displayed during an entire unit so students can refer to the words being studied.

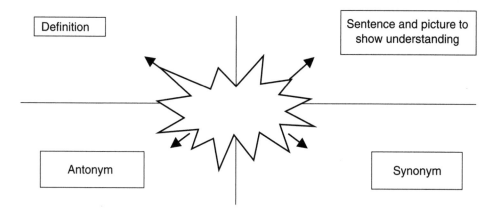

#37: TRACKING
PROGRESS WITH WORDS

When learning new spelling or vocabulary words, it is helpful for students to know exactly what the teacher expects of their usage. Tracking Progress With New Words makes such expectations clear. Make copies of the grid in Figure 2.10 and disseminate a fresh copy at the beginning of each week or at the outset of an instructional unit. Students and teachers can respond to each item in different colored pens to compare perceptions of word knowledge and use.

Figure 2.10   Vocabulary Progress Grid

Word Strategy	Poor	Fair	Good
Spelling of new words			
Written definitions of new words			
Identification of synonyms			
Identification of antonyms			
Use of words in written work			
Use of words in speaking			

#38: IMPROVING READING COMPREHENSION

Many studies show that reading skills improve when students use cognitive strategies to improve their comprehension (Cawelti, 1999). Achievement gains have also been observed when students actively discuss their reading with others through sharing, asking questions, and explaining. The strategic reading activity that follows can be applied to the reading of fiction and nonfiction materials across subject matter areas.

Questions to Consider Before Reading

- What is the topic?
- What do I already know about it?
- Why am I reading?
- What do I hope to learn or gain?
- What does the cover of the book tell me?
- What does the title suggest?
- What do the chapter headings suggest?
- What predictions can I make about the content?

Questions to Consider During Reading

- What is happening or what am I learning about?
- What are the most important facts or parts of the story?
- How does the structure of the text help me understand its ideas?
- Can I create images or words for the key ideas?
- What is confusing to me?
- Which words are new?
- What strategies can I use to understand the new words? Sound them out?
- Look at the pictures for clues. Figure out what makes sense.
- How would I summarize what I have read so far?
- Did my earlier predictions come true?
- What do I think will happen next?

Questions to Consider After Reading

- What information did I learn?
- What are some examples?
- How does this story relate to . . . ?
- How does this information expand my knowledge of . . . ?
- What were the most important points?
- Did my predictions come true? Why or why not?
- Are there parts I should reread?
- What do I have questions about?
- What is my opinion of what I just read?

#39: READING NONFICTION TEXTS

The skills for reading nonfiction vary from those for fiction. Teaching the structure of nonfiction texts helps students learn to read for different purposes and to vary their strategies accordingly. Figure 2.11 is a worksheet for finding the common components of nonfiction books. Once students have found the items on the worksheet, discuss how each item supports learning from nonfiction texts.

Figure 2.11   Reading Worksheet

Student Directions for Reading Nonfiction Books

Find the following items in your book. Write down the page numbers for each item on the list. After you have found examples of each item, discuss with the class how each nonfiction text feature helps you understand what is written.

Page	Nonfiction Book Item	How It Helps
_____	Title of book	_____
_____	Copyright date	_____
_____	Table of contents	_____
_____	Headings	_____
_____	Subheadings	_____
_____	Diagram and label	_____
_____	Picture or drawing	_____
_____	Caption	_____
_____	Index	_____
_____	References	_____
_____	Glossary	_____
_____	Appendix	_____

#40: A DAY'S DOSE OF DIVISION

Research shows that American students receive 30 minutes or fewer of math instruction per day (Cawelti, 1999). By increasing students' opportunities to learn math, achievement gains can be substantial. Some K-8 teachers are dedicating an entire school day to teaching a single math concept. While the strategy that follows features division, the same basic approach can be used with multiplication, probability, addition, fractions, and percentages. A Day's Dose can be implemented in a single class or schoolwide. You will need to invite two guest speakers on division and organize enough learning centers to accommodate three to four students at each. During the morning, students will visit two different center on one-digit dividing, and two additional centers on remainders. In all, you will need to plan four different center activities for a Day's Dose.

A Day's Dose of Division

9:00   Welcome students and any guests who have arrived. Explain goals and day's agenda.

9:15   Conduct math warm-ups—students stand while you ask them to stretch half of their bodies, bend half, and crumble a third.

9:25   Introduce guest presenter (parents, principal, high school student) to talk about the importance of division inside and outside school.

9:40   Host question and answer session with presenter.

9:50   Provide direct instruction on one-digit divisors.

10:05   Divide students into small groups of three to four for center work on one-digit divisors. Students work at the centers for 20 minutes and then rotate to the next center where they work for an additional 20 minutes.

10:45   Gather groups together. Debrief students about what they learned and their favorite center activities. Provide a brief break.

11:05   Provide direct instruction on remainders.

11:20   Assign students to work at centers on remainders in math for 20 minutes. They switch to second center for another 20 minutes.

12:00   Gather groups together and debrief.

12:10   Lunch and recess

12:50   Read aloud—division story (*The Doorbell Rang* by P. Hutchins)

1:20   Explain creative divisors—students can reenact story dramatically, visually, or through writing. Break them into small groups according to their choices.

2:00   Gather for whole-group sharing of creative divisors

2:20   Introduce second guest speaker on how division is used at work.

2:35   Host question-and-answer session with guest presenter.

2:45   Celebrate day's events. Assign division homework and dismiss at 3:00.

#41: ESTIMATION EXPLANATIONS

Estimation is an essential math skill because it is used more frequently than calculating exact numbers. It serves as an important referent in determining the reasonableness of numbers. Figure 2.12 is a chart of the most common estimation strategies and examples. Give this chart to students, provide them with items to estimate, and ask which strategies they rely on most frequently.

Figure 2.12 Estimation Skills

Rounding	Front End	Compatible Numbers	Others Developed by Students
236 200	420	36	
398 400	324	12 100	
+ 103 + 100	+ 229	62 100	
	??	81	
??? 700		+ 20	
(Estimate)	Estimate =		
	1) 420 = 400	Estimate = 220	
	2) 324 = 300		
	3) 229 = 250		
	4) 750 = Estimate		

Estimation explanations to give:

1. Estimate the number of first graders at your school.

2. Estimate the number of days you have lived.

3. Estimate how many breaths you take in an hour.

4. Estimate the number of cars in the school's parking lot.

5. Using the chart above, write estimation examples for subtraction.

6. Using the chart above, write estimation examples for division.

7. Using the chart above, write estimation examples for multiplication.

8. Invent your own estimation problems, and switch with another student.

9. Invent your own estimation strategies, and explain them to the class.

SOURCE: P. R. Trafton (n.d)

#42: CONSIDERING DIVERSE PERSPECTIVES

An important role of any social studies curriculum is to help students understand democratic values, to value the role of diversity in a democratic society, and to reduce discrimination. Reviews of research indicate that developing reasoning skills can prevent narrow either-or thinking (Shavel, 1999). Figure 2.13 asks students to consider diverse perspectives as well as common meeting grounds to enhance their respect for others.

Figure 2.13 Role Playing Current Events From Diverse Perspectives

Follow conflict-ridden stories in the local, national, or international news. Select several of these stories, enough for small groups of three students each. Give each group one of the articles and proceed through the following steps:

Step 1: Assign the three students per group a role each from among the following: Reader, Perspective #1, and Perspective #2.

Step 2: The Reader reads the article, and the group identifies the central conflict and at least two contrasting perspectives.

Step 3: Perspective #1 and Perspective #2 discuss the conflicts from their points of view. The Reader may step in to reread any portion of the article that warrants clarification.

Step 4: After both sides of the conflict have been articulated, ask the groups to make copies of the following chart. Tell them to specify the main points of view held by those role-playing Perspectives #1 and #2 and write their concerns in the first and third columns. Furthermore, ask the groups to identify any points the two sides hold in common and write these in the middle column.

Perspective #1	Common Ground	Perspective #2
Concern #1		Concern #1
Concern #2		Concern #2

Step 5: Have the groups discuss tentative ideas they might have for a win/win resolution to the conflict.

Step 6: The Readers from each group briefly summarize their group's work for the rest of the class.

#43: GETTING HISTORICAL

Instead of myriad dates, names, and events, history can be brought alive by choosing major issues in any identified period. Students can actively learn about issues in greater depth and take responsibility for teaching them to their peers. This strategy is a process for teaching historical periods in an 11-day format. To begin, select an historical period for study. Examples from U.S. history might include the westward expansion, the industrial revolution, the Civil War, or the 1960s.

Day 1

Begin the unit with a teacher-directed lesson on the period. As you teach the lesson, identify key ideas about the period and possible topics for students to consider researching at a later date.

Day 2

Teach a second lesson about the period and assign a reading selection for homework. Tell students that they must identify on a slip of paper 10 key ideas from their reading about the period. For students who have trouble reading, develop a phone buddy system for student volunteers to call one another to assist with the assignment.

Day 3

Discuss the 10 key ideas the students learned about the period from their reading. As you do, again point out possible research topics. Assign another reading, or Internet research assignment, where students must write a 100-word summary of the period.

Day 4

Organize students into mixed-ability groups of three or four. Ask them to share their summaries with their group members. After everyone has done so, tell the groups to create visuals illustrating what they think they know about the period at this point in their studies. The visuals could be flowcharts, classification charts, timelines, or mindmaps. Ask students to present their visuals to the rest of the class and discuss them as they do so.

Day 5

Show students a video addressing the topic they are studying. Ask them to compare the video's content with what they have learned so far. Ask students to write a brief summary of how the video deepened their knowledge of the period.

Day 6

Put students into the same mixed-ability groups as on Day 4. Tell the groups that they must select one aspect of the historical period to research. Their research must describe their topic, its significance in the historical period, its impact on society, and its similarity to current events. The groups are also responsible for including one visual in their presentation and for writing one essay question that will ultimately contribute to a class test. Tell students that the groups will present their research findings in 2 to 3 days, and allow them to decide whether they will present the first or second day. Each person in the group must have a contributing role. Also inform them that the next day will be spent in the school library researching their topics.

Day 7

Take the students to the school library for a research day, and assist those who appear to need guidance.

Days 8 and 9

Have the groups give their presentations and turn in their essay questions written on Day 6.

Day 10

Give the class test on the historic period. As part of the test, each group draws an essay question out of a hat. All the students in a group receive the same question but must respond individually. For homework, the members of the group who wrote the essay question must grade at least one response each and write a rationale for their grade. The teacher grades the rest of the test.

Day 11

Students meet with their peer evaluators to discuss the grades and what they learned. The teacher adjudicates any problems or unfair evaluations that may arise.

#44: THINKING SCIENTIFICALLY

Meaningful science curriculum seeks to develop the thinking necessary for scientific endeavors. The minidictionary below provides teachers and students with questions that nurture scientific thinking. These questions can be applied in the science classroom and throughout the curriculum.

A Minidictionary of Scientific Thinking Processes From A to V

- Analyzing

  What are the basic elements of this?
  What are some underlying assumptions?

- Asking questions

  What information do we need?
  What do we wonder about?

- Classifying

  How can we organize these into categories?
  What common characteristics do they share?

- Communicating

  How can we explain these objects, events, or ideas?
  What is the best way to get this across to someone?

- Comparing

  How are these items similar?
  In what ways are these items different?

- Connecting

  How does this relate to that?
  What is the cause and effect in this situation?

- Contrasting

  How do these items differ?
  What are the distinguishing characteristics of these items?

- Elaborating

  What would be an example of that?
  What other ideas or details could we add?
  How did we arrive at this?

- Evaluating

  What do you think about this and why?
  How well does this achieve the goal?

- Inferring

  What are the logical consequences of this?
  What conclusions can we make?

- Interpreting

  How might we explain?
  How can we describe?

- Measuring

  How can we determine its size?
  What tools can we use to determine its dimensions?

- Observing

  What do we notice?
  What else are we looking for?

- Operationalizing

  How can we put this into action?
  What do we need to do to study this?

- Pattern finding

  What is similar about these items?
  What repetition do you see in this?

- Predicting

  What do you think will happen?
  How do you know?
  Why is that likely?

- Sequencing

  How can these items be arranged in a linear way?
  What should go first, second, and third?

- Summarizing

  How can we retell that in a shortened form?
  What did we learn?

- Synthesizing

  What emerges when we combine these ideas?
  Overall, what is evident?

- Verifying

  What evidence is there to support this?
  How can we confirm or prove this?

#45: CONDUCTING SCIENTIFIC INQUIRY

Scientific inquiry is a method of approaching problems; it is used by professional scientists or anyone interested in seeking answers to questions about everyday life. The process involves a number of distinct components, but they do not necessarily proceed in a lockstep manner. The following components provide guidance for organizing experiments to ensure worthwhile learning and achievement.

Components of Scientific Inquiry

Asking Questions. The students or teacher express curiosity about a natural phenomenon. Students discuss what they think they know about the topic and identify questions to explore. The problem or question to be researched should be clearly identified.

Gathering Data. Students gather data, conduct observations, and begin to propose hypotheses or explanations for their questions. Data should be organized and recorded as the students proceed.

Analyzing Data. Students review their data and look for patterns or trends. At this stage, using graphic displays of data is helpful for noting pattern formations.

Making Predictions. Students suggest a cause or theory to explain their findings.

Reflecting. Students review their procedures, look for errors, and consider the types of problem-solving skills they used and what would improve their experiments next time.

Sharing Findings. Students present their studies, identifying their original questions, what they learned, and how they would improve on their efforts next time.

SUGGESTED READINGS
FOR FURTHER INFORMATION

Campbell, L., & Campbell, B. (1999). *Multiple Intelligences and Student Achievement: Success Stories from Six Schools.* Alexandria, VA: Association for Supervision and Curriculum Development.

In a case-study format, this book explores the impact of Gardner's theory of MI on student achievement. The book chronicles how two elementary, two middle-level, and two senior high schools use MI theory in their programs and the resultant achievement gains of their students. In addition to surveying instruction, curriculum, and assessment methods used at each of the six schools, the book also describes unexpected findings about the ability of MI theory to positively influence teacher, student, and parent beliefs about what is possible in learning.

Cawelti, G. (Ed.). (1999). *Handbook of Research on Improving Student Achievement* (2nd ed.). Arlington, VA: Educational Research Service.

This book surveys classroom practices that research has shown result in higher student achievement. The book's core premise is that efforts to improve teaching must be anchored in the existing knowledge base. Twelve well-known subject-matter experts each contribute a chapter to the book. Each chapter, formatted similarly, gives an overview of the content area, a summary of the research findings, on effective instructional practices, implications for the classroom, and references. The scope of the book is broad and includes the arts, foreign language, health, language arts, oral communication, mathematics, physical education, science, social studies, generic practices, and staff development.

Zemelson, S., Daniels, H., & Hyde, A. (1998). *Best Practice: New Standards for Teaching and Learning in America's Schools* (2nd ed.). Portsmouth, NH: Heinemann.

This book summarizes the major national standards projects since 1993. It offers descriptions of best practices in six subject areas: reading, writing, mathematics, science, social studies, and the arts, and provides vignettes of actual teachers and their exemplary classroom practices. The book asserts that students learn best in schools that are student centered, experiential, democratic, collaborative, and rigorously challenging.

REFERENCES

American Association of School Administrators. (2001). *An educator's guide to school-wide reform.* Retrieved August 2, 2002, from www.aasa.org/issues_and_insights/district_organization/Reform/overview.htm

Beck, I., & McKeown, M. (1981, Nov.-Dec.). Developing questions that promote comprehension: The story map. *Language Arts,* 913-918.

Bransford, J. D., Brown, A. L., & Cocking, R. R. (Eds.). (1999). *How people learn: Brain, mind, experience, and school.* Washington, DC: National Academy Press.

Campbell, B. (1994). The multiple intelligences handbook: Lesson plans and more. Standwood, WA: Campbell & Associates.

Campbell, L., & Campbell, B. (1999). *Multiple intelligences and student achievement: Success stories from six schools.* Alexandria, VA: Association for Supervision and Curriculum Development.

Campbell, L., Campbell, B., & Dickinson, D. (1999). *Teaching and learning through multiple intelligences*, 2nd Ed. Boston, MA: Allyn & Bacon.

Cawelti, G. (Ed.). (1999). *Handbook of research on improving student achievement* (2nd ed.). Arlington, VA: Educational Research Service.

D'Arcangelo, M. (2000, November). The scientist in the crib: A conversation with Andrew Meltzoff. *Educational Leadership, 58*(3), 8-13.

Darling-Hammond, L. (1996). *What matters most: Teaching for America's future.* Woodbridge, VA: National Commission on Teaching and America's Future.

Diamond, M., & Hopson, J. (1998). *Magic trees of the mind: How to nurture your child's intelligence, creativity, and healthy emotions from birth through adolescence.* New York: Penguin.

Dunn, R., & Dunn, K. (1978). *Teaching students through their individual learning styles: A Practical approach.* Boston, MA: Allyn & Bacon.

Frisk, E. (Ed.) (1999). *Champions of change: The impact of the arts on learning.* Washington, DC: The Arts Education Partnership and The President's Committee on the Arts and Humanities.

Gardner, H. (1983). *Frames of mind: The theory of multiple intelligences.* New York: Basic Books.

Gardner, H. (1995, November). Reflections on multiple intelligences: Myths and messages. *Phi Delta Kappan,* 200-209.

Glasser, W. (1990, February). The quality school. *Phi Delta Kappan, 71*(6), 424-435.

Howard, B. C. (1987). *Learning to persist: Persisting to learn* [training program]. Washington DC: Mid-Atlantic Center for Race Equity, American University.

Hutchins, P. (1989). *The doorbell rang.* Parsippany: NJ: Pearson Learning.

Klausmeier, H. J. (1985). *Educational psychology* (5th ed.). New York: Harper & Row.

Kuykendall, C. (1991). *Improving black student achievement* [training program]. Chevy Chase, MD: Mid-Atlantic Equity Consortium.

Marzano, R., Pickering, J., & Pollock, J. (2001). *Classroom instruction that works.* Alexandria, VA: Association for Supervision and Curriculum Development.

Missouri Department of Elementary and Secondary Education. (1998). *MI way of learning.* Retrieved August 9, 2002, from www.successlink.org/best/b7.html

Ramirez, M., III, & Casteneda, A. (1974). *Cultural democracy: Bicognitive development and education.* New York: Academic Press.

Shade, B. J. (1989). *Culture, style, and the educative process.* Springfield, IL: Charles C. Thompson.

Shavel, J. P. (1999). Social studies. In G. Cawelti (Ed.), *Handbook on research on improving student achievement* (2nd ed.). Arlington, VA: Educational Research Service.

Shulman, L. (1987). Knowledge and teaching: Foundations of the new reform. *Harvard Educational Review, 57,* 1-22.

Tharp, R. (1994). Intergroup differences among Native Americans in socialization and child cognition: An ethnogenetic analysis. In P. Greenfield and R. Cocking (Eds.), *Cross-cultural roots of minority child development* (pp. 87-105). Hillsdale, NJ: Lawrence Erlbaum.

Trafton, P. R. (n.d.). *National Science Foundation Estimation Project.* Retrieved August 3, 2002, from University of Idaho, ivc.uidaho. edu/ed326/resources/est_strategies. html

Witkin, H. A., Moore, C. A., Goodenough, D. R., & Cox, P. W. (1977). Field-dependent and field-independent cognitive styles and their educational implications. *Review of Educational Research, 47,* 1-64.

Zemelman, S., Daniels, H., & Hyde, A. (1998*). Best practice: New standards for teaching and learning in America's schools* (2nd ed.). Portsmouth, NH: Heinemann.

3

Ensuring Gender-Fair Instruction

For Female and Male Students

Assigned to the same classroom and taught by the same teacher, boys and girls receive different educations. During the 1990s, research into this phenomenon caused gender equity to emerge as a prominent educational concern. At first, attention centered on how schools discriminated against girls. Girls were portrayed as invisible in school curriculum, behind boys in math and science achievement, overlooked by well-meaning teachers, sufferers of low self-esteem, and, eventually, of economic inequities (American Association of University Women Educational Foundation, 1992). Sadker and Sadker (1994) added additional descriptions of school-based discrimination. They reported that gender bias begins in elementary school, that girls are shortchanged in classroom discussions, on the playground, and throughout the curriculum. They also noted that although girls enroll in math and science classes more frequently than their male counterparts, they don't persist and are significantly outnumbered by boys in upper-division math and science classes such as calculus and physics.

More recently, attention has focused on discrimination against boys. Some assert that girls fare better than boys by many educational measures. Boys earn lower grades than girls; are disproportionately labeled as learning disabled and placed in special education programs; drop out of school in greater numbers; are more frequently involved in alcohol, drugs, and violent crimes; and have higher rates of suicide (Gurian, Henley, & Trueman, 2001; Sadker & Sadker, 2001; Sommers, 2000).

What causes the differences in male and female students' experiences of K-12 schooling? Researchers have suggested numerous reasons. They include:

1. Socialization processes and sex-role stereotyping (American Association of University Women [AAUW] Educational Foundation, 1992; Brown & Gilligan, 1992; Gilligan, 1982; Kindlon & Thompson, 1999; Sadker & Sadker, 1994; Tovey, 1995)

2. School curricula and differential treatment by teachers (AAUW, 1992, 1998; Mid-Atlantic Equity Center, 1993; Sadker & Sadker, 2001)

3. A lack of mentors and role models, discrimination, and low self-confidence (Brown & Gilligan, 1992; Education Review Office, 2000; Kindlon & Thompson, 1999)

4. The role of sex differences in brain chemistry (Gurian, Henley, & Trueman, 2001)

Table 3.1 provides a snapshot of the educational impact of such inequities regardless of the reasons for sexism in the schools. The table's data were compiled from a variety of sources: AAUW, 1998; Devon County Council (UK), 2000; Educational Development Corporation, 1999; Education Review Office, 2000; Kindlon & Thompson, 1999; Mid-Atlantic Equity Center, 1999; Sadker & Sadker, 2001; Sommers, 2000.

THE EDUCATIONAL ADVANTAGES AND DISADVANTAGES OF FEMALE AND MALE STUDENTS

It is clear that inequity can and does work in both directions. Male and female students suffer from gender bias in schools. As a recent AAUW (1998) report stated, "When equity is the goal, all gaps in performance warrant attention, regardless [of] whether they disadvantage boys or girls." Both genders need and deserve K-12 experiences that promote high academic achievement. How can this be accomplished?

PROMOTING GENDER EQUITY IN THE CLASSROOM

There are several actions teachers can take to promote equitable achievement. First, we can begin by scrutinizing ourselves. No educator chooses to treat students inequitably, and we are typically unaware of discriminatory classroom dynamics. Research in the late 1990s found that teachers receive little training in gender equity and, as a result, may inadvertently reinforce sex biases in the classroom (AAUW, 1998; Bullock, 1997; Campbell & Sanders, 1997). Some researchers suggest that teaching practices will become more equitable if teachers reflect on their interactions with female and male students (Bullock, 1997;

Table 3.1   Educational Advantages and Disadvantages of Male and Female
Students

Issue	Girls	Boys
Extracurricular Activities	More girls participate in school government, school clubs, and the performing arts than boys.	Boys outnumber girls in school sports, and such programs are better financed.
Literacy	Girls perform better in reading and writing and take more English classes. Yet boys score better in English on most college-bound tests.	Boys significantly underperform girls in reading and writing and take fewer English courses. They outnumber girls in remedial English.
Math and Science	In elementary school, girls perform equally with boys in math. Though K-12 enrollment in math and science classes has increased, girls do not often participate in advanced programs or score well on advanced-placement (AP) tests.	Boys take more advanced courses in math, biology, chemistry, and physics. More score well on AP tests.
Technology	Girls infrequently take computer science and technology classes, especially in Grades 8 to 11. They often enroll in word processing and clerical support classes.	Boys take more technology classes and enroll in more advanced technology courses. They exhibit higher computer self-confidence than girls.
Overall Academics	Girls study harder and earn higher grades.	Boys receive lower grades and repeat a grade more frequently.
Test Scores	In early grades, girls outperform boys on achievement tests, but their performance declines through high school. On the American College Test (ACT), girls score higher in English while boys score higher in math. The same is true on the National Assessment of Education Progress (NAEP).	Boys score far lower in literacy skills than girls on K-12 achievement tests, but they score higher in verbal and math skills on the SAT. They also score higher in math, science, history, and geography on the NAEP.
Classroom Discipline	Girls tend to be quieter, cause fewer discipline problems, interact less with teachers, be asked fewer complex questions, and receive less praise and constructive feedback than boys. They are not disciplined as harshly as boys for similar offenses.	Boys tend to be louder, dominate class discussions, be more physically active, and receive more teacher attention. They comprise the majority of school discipline problems. Also, they are disciplined more harshly, more publicly, and more frequently than girls.

(Continued)

Table 3.1 (*Continued*)

Issue	Girls	Boys
Behavioral and Learning Disorders	Girls suffer from low self-esteem, stress, depression, and eating disorders more frequently than boys.	Hyperactivity is far greater among boys. Boys exhibit more learning disabilities, reading problems, and mental retardation than girls.
Drop-Out Rates	Girls who repeat grades drop out more often than boys who do so. Teen pregnancy is frequently cited as a common reason to quit school.	The majority of school dropouts are boys, and this is often attributed to the mismatch between boys and school norms.
Educational Goals	Slightly more college students are female; however, girls believe they will have a more difficult time attaining their goals than boys.	Males are the minority in college at both the bachelor's and master's levels. Yet, more males earn PhDs than females.
Violence	Girls are more frequently victimized by sexual harassment and abuse. Many incidents go unreported, and girls tend to suffer more damaging consequences than boys.	Boys are victims of violence at school more often than girls, take part in more bullying, sexual harassment, weapon carrying, hate crime attacks, and school shootings.

Gay, 1989). Since it has been estimated that teachers have up to 1,000 interactions with students in a single day (Bullock, 1997), there is ample opportunity for behavior to speak more loudly than words. Clinical observations and honest self-assessment can uncover the disparate educational experiences of boys and girls. Once informed about our attitudes and behaviors, we can seek to modify them.

A second approach to reducing gender disparity is to take stock of the curriculum materials we use. Studies suggest that students spend as much 80% to 95% of their time using textbooks, and that most teachers' instructional decisions are based on textbooks (Hulme, 1988; Woodward & Elliot, 1990). Though some progress has been made in developing nonsexist materials, making today's texts less biased than those of 20 years ago, they nevertheless are not bias-free. For example, in the basic-skills disciplines of language arts, math, social studies, and science, more males than females are represented in the text and illustrations (Bazler & Simons, 1990; Educational Development Corporation, 1999; Sadker & Sadker, 1994). This under-representation communicates that women as a group are less important in society. By knowing what to look for, teachers can assess the texts they use to identify inequities and supplement them as appropriate. In this chapter, I suggest strategies for doing so.

Gender-fair instructional materials are not enough, however, to create an equitable learning environment. Finally, attention must be given to daily instructional processes. Research has demonstrated ways to increase academic success for both genders, and several of these strategies are included in this chapter. Examples of these techniques follow: higher-level thinking strategies (Haggerty, 1991); cooperative learning (Arnow, 1995; Slavin, 1990); competitive learning (Devon County Council [UK], 2000; Goldstein, Haldane, & Mitchell, 1990); the use of language, movement, and manipulatives to improve reading (Devon County Council [UK], 2000; Education Review Office, 2000); and making science, math, and technology classrooms more girl-friendly, so females are better prepared for future profitable career opportunities (Arnow, 1995; Bullock, 1997).

While gender bias continues to influence the education of all students, teachers, nevertheless, can make an enormous difference in their classrooms. This chapter supports such efforts with three types of techniques: teacher self-reflection, assessment of gender bias in curricular materials, and gender-fair instruction. We have taken care to avoid pitting one gender-centered model against the other. Instead, we suggest that everyone can benefit from an expanded notion of learning and teaching. Ultimately, the way each student learns is highly idiosyncratic. As teachers, we can become adept observers of our students and accommodate them for the individuals they are.

#46: CONDUCTING
A PERSONAL GENDER AUDIT

Gender bias exists because we all are socialized to treat girls and boys differently. The first step in promoting equity is to become aware of our own biased behaviors and change them. The gender bias audit or inventory in Figure 3.1 asks you to reflect on several classroom dynamics. Rate yourself (or ask a colleague to observe you), noting what you would most like to change about your instruction.

Figure 3.1 Teacher Rating on Gender Issues

Equity Issue	Often	Sometimes	Could Improve
Environmental Considerations			
1. Males and females are equally represented in bulletin boards, posters, and wall decorations.			
2. Classroom visuals portray males in nurturing roles.			
3. Classroom visuals portray females in active roles.			
4. Work samples of girls and boys are displayed equally.			
5. Books in the classroom library feature females and males in nontraditional roles.			
Teacher Behaviors			
6. Gender-fair language is used. Exclusive *she* or *he* references to roles such as nurses or mechanics are avoided.			
7. Wait time of 5 to 10 seconds is provided after asking a question.			
8. Language, voice, tone, and nonverbals are monitored for sexist generalizations.			
9. The same amount and type of casual conversation occurs with male and female students.			
10. Teacher requests for help are equitably assigned to female and male students.			
11. Girls and boys are called on equally in class.			
12. Classroom disrupters receive similar responses from the teacher.			
13. Boys and girls are seated in the classroom according to relevant rationales.			
Instructional Strategies			
14. Higher-level questions are alternated between male and female students.			
15. Active, hands-on learning is provided to all students.			
16. Classwork is accomplished in cross-gender groupings.			
17. Curricular materials feature both genders in a wide variety of roles.			
18. Female and male role models are highlighted in course materials and classroom guests.			
19. Specific, constructive feedback is offered to all students.			

#47: SEEKING STUDENT FEEDBACK ON GENDER DYNAMICS

Figure 3.2 was developed for teachers who want to learn how students experience gender dynamics in the classroom.

Figure 3.2 Student Rating on Gender Issues

Teacher's Name: _____

Class Name: _____ Date: _____

I am a (check one): _____ Female student _____ Male student

Please check the response that fits you the best:	Never	Sometimes	Often
The Classroom Environment			
1. Pictures on the walls show boys and girls equally.			
2. Both boys' and girls' work is posted for everyone to see.			
3. There are an equal number of books and other reading materials for boys and girls.			
4. I feel welcome in this class.			
5. I feel invisible or unappreciated in this class.			
6. The teacher talks to me as much as to others in the class.			
7. The teacher expects me to do my best in this class.			
8. The teacher expects all others to do their best in this class.			
Teaching and Learning Experiences			
9. We learn from teacher lectures.			
10. We learn through whole-class discussions.			
11. We learn through hands-on activities.			
12. We learn cooperatively in small groups.			
13. We learn by working alone.			
14. The teacher calls on girls to respond to questions.			
15. The teacher calls on boys to respond to questions.			
16. I am interrupted when I speak in class.			
17. The teacher gives me enough time to respond to questions.			
18. The teacher is fair with me if I misbehave.			
19. The teacher is fair with others if they misbehave.			
20. The teacher helps all of us with assignments equally.			

My favorite way to learn is _____

One thing I would change to make the class better for girls is _____

_____

One thing I would change to make this class better for boys is _____

_____

One thing I would change to make this class better for me is _____

_____

#48: ASSESSING BIAS IN CURRICULAR MATERIALS

For teachers to detect bias in instructional materials, it is necessary to recognize many forms of bias. It also must be acknowledged that bias is not limited to gender issues and can include race, age, abilities, class, language background, and sexual orientation. Sadker & Sadker (2001) have identified seven forms of bias that are often evident in educational materials. Figure 3.3 adapts the Sadkers' information and can serve as a tool for assessing whether bias is evident in curricular materials.

Figure 3.3 Rating Gender Bias in Instructional Materials

Title of instructional resource: _____

Form of Bias	No Bias Evident	Bias Evident	Ways to Reduce Bias
Omission—males and females are not equally featured in text and illustrations			
Sexist Language—masculine pronouns and terms such as *mankind* and *forefathers* are used			
Stereotyping—the genders are portrayed in "traditional" roles, such as male heavy-equipment operators and female nurses			
Imbalance—minimal information is given on important issues, e.g., one paragraph explains the suffrage movement in the United States			
Unreality—controversial topics are ignored in favor of traditional views, e.g., avoidance of divorce statistics when describing families			
Fragmentation—groups are portrayed in a fragmented or clustered fashion so that all women writers are featured together rather than integrated throughout			
Cosmetic Bias—efforts are made to have materials look balanced when only minimal coverage is actually offered			

SOURCE: Adapted from Sadker & Sadker (2001).

#49: QUALITY QUESTIONING

The questions teachers ask place different cognitive demands on students. All students should have opportunities to consider and respond to higher-level questions. The following question strips can be photocopied for easy referencing during class. A word of caution is in order. Wait five seconds before asking a student to respond to one of these questions to increase the quality of thinking.

Questions for Analytical Thinking

How is this . . . related to . . . ?
Can you organize or sort this into categories?
What relationships exist among . . . ?
Can you outline or diagram . . . . ?
What patterns do you discern?
What does this remind you of?
Can you put this into a sequence?
Can we order these into a hierarchy?
What is the key concept?
What are supporting details?
What is irrelevant?
How would you compare . . . to . . . ?
How might you contrast this . . . with . . . ?
What conclusions can be drawn from . . . ?
What appears to be the cause of . . . . ?
What are the results of . . . ?
What do you predict will occur?
How did you arrive at that?
How should we proceed?
What can you do with this information?
Can you tell me more?

Questions for Critical Thinking

What examples can you give?
What alternatives might exist?
What questions do you have?
What steps can we take to . . . ?
What information do we need to decide?
What conclusion can you draw?
What is an explanation for . . . ?
Do you agree with . . . ?
Why? How do you know?
What choice would you have made?
What might happen if . . . ?
What evidence supports . . . ?
What is a likely outcome? Why?
What are the advantages or disadvantages of . . . ?
Whose point of view is evident?
Is this information bias-free?
What are some unstated assumptions?
What is the theme or message?

Questions for Evaluative Thinking

What is your opinion of . . . ? Why?
Why did he or she choose to . . . ?
What was most or least effective?
What would you recommend?
What standards could we develop to assess . . . ?
What criteria would you use to determine . . . ?
How well does this meet the goals?
How would you prove or disprove . . . ?
How do we know this evidence is reliable?
What evidence exists . . . for . . . ?
What is the importance of . . . ?
What is your conclusion?
Would it be better if . . . ?
What choice would you have made?
Who might disagree with you and why?
What advantages and disadvantages exist?
How do the results compare to the criteria?
Were the requirements met?
What value does this have?

#50: USING NONSEXIST LANGUAGE

Nonsexist language is referred to as gender-neutral or inclusive language. It treats females and males equitably. Because English has no generic singular, we typically use *he, his,* and *him* in common expressions such as *the student . . . he.* This pervasive use of the masculine pronoun excludes women from a variety of roles. Suggestions for how to use nonsexist language follow; they make simple changes to personal pronouns and commonly used, everyday nouns.

Personal Pronouns

1. Reword in plural form.

Examples	*Replacements*
He must turn in his assignment.	Students should turn in their assignments.
The counselor will schedule his own appointment.	The counselors will schedule their appointments.

2. Eliminate gender references.

Examples	*Replacements*
No one should leave her car unlocked.	Cars should be locked.
He must return it by that date.	It must be returned by that date.

3. Alternate female and male references (sparingly).

Examples	*Replacements*
Encourage each child to attend as she is able.	Encourage each child to attend as he is able.
Has he been able to do so?	Has she been able to do so?
Did he contribute?	Did she contribute?

Table 3.2   Replacing Sexist With Nonsexist Language

Nouns: Students might go on a word search to add to this list.

Instead of:	*Use:*
actress	actor
brotherhood	human family
businessman	businessperson
chairman	chairperson
coed	student
cleaning lady	housekeeper, janitor
congressman	member of congress, representative
fireman	firefighter
founding fathers	founding leaders
housewife	homemaker
mailman	postal worker, mail deliverer
manhood	adulthood
mankind	humanity
manmade	synthetic, handmade
manpower	personnel, staff
middleman	go-between, intermediary
newsman	reporter
policeman	police officer
repairman	technician, mechanic, electrician
salesman	salesperson
sisterhood	human family
spokesman	spokesperson
sportsman	athlete
stewardess	flight attendant
watchman	security guard
workman	worker

#51: THINKING WHILE LISTENING

Boys and girls approach learning from somewhat different perspectives and with slightly different needs. Many girls tend to use a conversational style, share ideas that build on one another, and seek consensus. Cooperative learning complements these inherent strengths while also tapping the interests of peer-based learning among boys. Thinking While Listening is particularly effective for use with worksheets and while practicing skills.

1. Identify a collaborative skill students should practice. Sample skills include using appropriate behavior, staying on task, paraphrasing or summarizing, using effective listening skills, or critiquing ideas appropriately.

2. Divide students into small groups of about four. You may want to have students count off in numbers from one to four and cluster ones, twos, threes, and fours together respectively.

3. Provide each group with a worksheet or assignment.

4. Select one problem from the assignment. Model thinking through the problem out loud with students observing your efforts. Ask students for feedback on your thinking process, on whether your response was accurate and effective, and why or why not. Be sure that all students understand the procedures they are to use.

5. Instruct the group members to divide the problems equally among themselves. Also remind them of the collaborative skill they are practicing.

6. Each student takes a turn solving a problem. Group members concurrently encourage and evaluate one another's efforts.

7. After all group members have taken their turns, give the groups time to determine that every member understands all the problems. Also, have them reflect on how effectively they use the collaborative skill.

8. If desired, give students a new assignment sheet with similar problems. Have them complete the second assignment individually as an accountability measure.

#52: MIX AND MATCH

The cooperative learning activity below assists students in developing expertise and teaching one another. It can be used with teacher-made information cards, with sections of an assigned chapter, or with entire chapters or books. It is based on the jigsaw technique originally developed by Aronson, Blaney, Stephan, Sikes, and Snapp (1978).

1. Organize materials into four sections, numbering each section, 1, 2, 3, and 4.

2. Cluster students into groups of four. Provide each group with the complete set of instructional materials divided into fourths. Explain that students must teach their peers about the content they each have received. Note, these groups are referred to as the master group.

3. To teach their groups, students must first learn their content. They do so by working with those who have the same information. Organize students so that all the ones are together in a group, all the twos are together in another, and so on. (See Figure 3.3.)

4. The expert groups develop strategies to teach their content.

5. The experts return to the master groups and teach the content.

Figure 3.3 Master and Expert Groupings

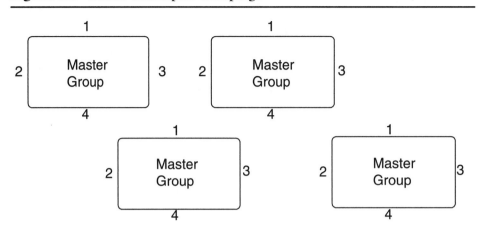

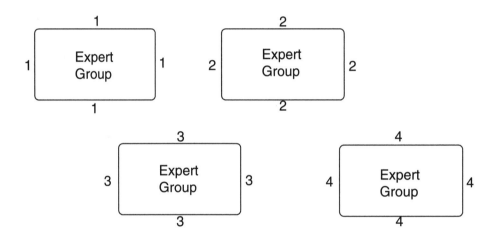

#53: FLASH CARD TAG

Some boys (and girls) respond well to classroom challenges and games. In addition to athletics, regular classrooms can occasionally feature contests, games, and competitive exercises to engage student interest and attention. Flash Card Tag, for example, can be used for any kind of classroom content that is available on flash cards, such as math, geographic facts, or spelling words.

Step 1: Place two equal sets of flash cards on two desks in the front of the room.

Step 2: Divide students into two groups of single-file lines facing forward. The first student from each team should be about 10 feet from the desk with the flash cards.

Step 3: Use a signal to begin play. The first student goes to the desk, takes the first flash card, holds it up, announces the answer to the class, places the card in a discard pile, and then tags the next person in line.

Step 4: If students do not know the answer or give an incorrect one, they must put the card on the bottom of the pile and select the next card. They will continue to select cards until they get a correct answer or until they have drawn four cards.

Step 5: The first team to correctly give the answer to all the flash cards wins.

#54: FAST-TRACKING THE MULTIPLICATION FACTS

This competitive game is adapted from the simple card game called War. You will need a deck of cards for every two players in the room. Before the game begins, write on an overhead that Ace = 1, J = 10, Q = 11, K = 12. Explain the steps as follows:

1. Organize students into pairs. Give each pair a deck of cards and ask them to shuffle the cards.

2. The pairs should divide their cards evenly among themselves, stacking the cards face down on their desks.

3. Both students turn over their top card at the same time. They multiply the two cards and shout out the answer. Students who call out the correct answer first add their teammate's cards to their pile. If a tie occurs, the pairs continue to turn over their cards until someone wins the pile.

4. When the original stack of cards has been played through, the pairs count their winnings. Whoever has the most cards wins a pencil, a point, or a round of applause. If another round of play is desired, partners can be switched.

#55: SEQUENCE CARDS

Many students, females and males alike, enjoy opportunities to physically engage with their learning, whether through touch or movement. Using sequence cards is a simple way to add tactile and kinesthetic components to learning.

Sequence cards are sets of four-by-six-inch notecards featuring a succession of words, numbers, events, steps, or other sequences. Sets of cards might include the parts of a sentence, numbers and symbols in a mathematical formula, historical events in chronological order, words or letters in alphabetical order, or steps in a process such as how a bill becomes law (see Figure 3.4). Hand out the cards randomly to students with the directions that all students who get a card go to the front of the class and put themselves in the proper order.

Figure 3.4 Sets of Sequence Cards

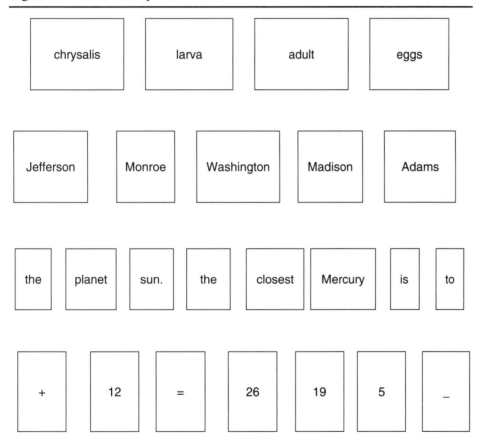

#56: PAPER PLATE REVIEW

This strategy engages students physically in recalling facts or concepts. The needed supplies are minimal: paper plates, marking pens, a paper clip, and information from a recent unit of study.

To do a paper plate review:

1. Choose 8 to 12 questions such as those in Figure 3.5, related to a topic of study.

2. Make a spinner. Put each question in one section of the spinner. A paper-clip makes a good pointer.

3. Write the answer to each question on three to four paper plates and spread them around the room face up.

4. One student spins and calls out the questions, while the remaining students touch a plate with the correct answer with a finger or foot.

5. Two rules are necessary. Students cannot touch anyone else, and they must be quiet enough to hear the questions.

Figure 3.5 Spinner for Paper Plate Review Game

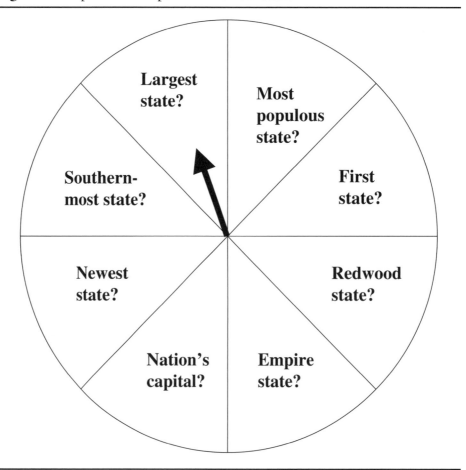

#57: HEADBANDS

Students (especially boys) like this game because they move around the room while trying to guess vocabulary words written on headbands they each wear. Classmates give clues about essential attributes, characteristics, or the qualities of a word or concept's meaning.

1. Identify several vocabulary words or concepts that you want to reinforce.

2. Put one word on a sentence strip. Staple the strips to make headbands.

3. Distribute headbands, asking the students to put them on without looking at the words. Some teachers place the headbands on backward so the student does not see the word; once on, the headband can be rotated.

4. When all students have their headbands on, they get up and walk around the room asking each other three questions to guess the word. This can be done in small groups. They can only ask each classmate one question at a time. The questions are:

   What classification of things does it fit into?

   What are its essential characteristics?

   What are some examples of it?

5. An example might be the word *antibody* from a science unit. Responses could be "substances to fight diseases," "antitoxins," or "the big police force of the body."

6. Give students enough time so most can guess their words. Then have them remove their headbands to check if their guesses were correct.

#58: A WORD TOOLKIT

Poor literacy impedes academic success and is a problem that confronts far too many boys (and girls, and adults for that matter!). Research suggests specific strategies to improve reading skills. These include smaller class sizes to assist poor readers, early diagnosis and intervention, daily reading time, reading materials that match each student's interests, and the scaffolding of complex tasks (Devon County Council [UK], 2000; Education Review Office, 2000). Some reading strategies target the scaffolding of complex reading tasks. A Word Toolkit teaches word attack skills, skills that are sorely needed among students who struggle with reading (Education Review Office, 2000).

A Word Toolkit

When you see a word you don't know, use the following word tools:

1. Sound it out.

2. Break the word into syllables.

3. Look for smaller words or word parts that you recognize.

4. Keep reading to see what makes sense.

5. Use the words around it to identify the meaning.

6. Think of a different word that makes sense.

7. Ask your partner.

8. Use a dictionary.

9. Guess and go on.

10. Ask your teacher.

11. Use picture clues.

12. Use the sounds of the first letters to get you going.

13. Add suffixes.

14. Consider whether you have seen the word before and what it meant then.

#59: BITE-SIZE READING

When students read textbooks, they encounter many tasks simultaneously. They find new words and information, key concepts, and supporting details, and they juggle these and other tasks in an effort to comprehend their reading assignments. The complexity of reading new content can become more manageable with bite-size pieces, especially for male students who struggle with reading. The following encourages students to interact with content in small amounts and then go back for more.

Step 1: Assign students to read silently for 15 minutes.

Step 2: Pair students up for 5 minutes to discuss what they just read. Sometimes it helps to ask the pair to make at least five notes.

Step 3: Teacher leads whole-class discussion on the main ideas and supporting details for 3 to 5 minutes.

Step 4: Students read silently for 10 to 15 minutes, and the process repeats itself.

This strategy can be adapted to include a visual component. Ask students to read short sections of text and then create visual symbols of what they read. Students can work in teams to translate their new knowledge into visual representations.

#60: READING ACROSS THE CONTENT AREAS

Many students struggle with reading in language arts courses and in other classes as well. Throughout this book, I have identified multiple strategies to improve reading skills. Here, I combine several and suggest additional strategies to help students read across the content areas.

Before Reading

- Use strategies from Chapter 1 to elicit prior knowledge such as #1: The Known and Unknown; #2: Things I Know, Think I Know, Want to Know; or #13: Guided Anticipation.
- Ask students to brainstorm or predict the content.
- Set reading goals.
- Preview new vocabulary with strategies such as #36: Vocabulary Word Savvy; #37: Tracking Progress With Words; or #57: Headbands.
- Teach students how to scan and highlight information.
- Show them—with Strategy #39: Reading Nonfiction Texts—how to work with nonfiction texts.

During Reading

- Log the content learned; use Strategy #19: Visually Tracking a Classroom Unit.
- Ask students to take notes with Strategy #16: Getting the Big Idea With Cue Cards.
- Use any of the Multiple Intelligence Strategies from #20 through #35 to teach specific concepts from the reading.
- Use cooperative learning techniques such as #52: Mix and Match.
- Break reading into manageable chunks of content; use #59: Bite-Size Reading.
- Ask students to make graphic organizers of the content, such as organizers shown in Strategy #4: Getting Organized Graphically; #5: Visual Sequencing; or #6: Visualizing Cause and Effect.

After Reading

- Ask students to make journal entries about their reading.
- Provide copies of Strategy #17: Visual Report Writing and ask students to write a report using the form as a guide.
- Give students copies of Strategy #35: It's Classified! and ask them to visually organize what they have learned.
- Encourage students to extend their learning through Strategy #33: Tapping Student Interests With Projects.
- Have students select any of the Multiple Intelligence Strategies #20 through 35 to demonstrate what they have learned in a mode of their choice.

#61: SIX TIPS FOR
TECH-SAVVY GIRLS

Girls constitute less than 20% of the students enrolled in advanced computer science courses, but they dominate the basic data-entry-level courses, thus preparing themselves for employment in lower-paying clerical work (AAUW, 1998). Girls are also less likely to use computers outside of school, and current software reinforces gender stereotypes. Research in the United States, Britain, Canada, and Australia show that computer science degrees for women have actually decreased over time (Women's Television Network Foundation [WTN], 2000). While discouraging, these trends are not the final word. The following tips can spark girls' interests in technology.

Tip #1. Present computers as a tool for creating and communicating, rather than as a machine to be programmed. You may also want to ask older girls to introduce the computer to students in lower grades.

Tip #2. Incorporate computer technology into numerous forms of course work, and use a variety of software programs including graphics, writing, and art programs.

Tip #3. Ensure that girls have equal access to computers. If computers are in labs, see if they might be moved into classrooms where boys will have fewer opportunities to dominate the equipment.

Tip #4. In the classroom, rather than using computers for free play, schedule equal time for female and male students. Also, limit game playing, which tends to attract boys, sometimes to the exclusion of girls.

Tip #5. Invite girls to form a committee to address technology inequities in the school. Specifically attempt to involve girls at critical stages, such as between sixth and eighth grade, a time of important decision making, when interest in technology wanes.

Tip #6. Encourage girls to navigate cyberspace with girl-friendly tools. Two helpful sites include the following:

> www.girltech.com (retrieved August 3, 2002): This interactive site provides information of interest to girls on a wide variety of subjects including sciences, careers, history, sports and the arts. It also provides links to other sites.

> ww.tomorrows-girl.com/ (retrieved August 3, 2002): This site showcases the achievements of girls in math, science, and technology while also providing links to other sites, such as Girl Power, Girls Using Real Life Science (G.U.R.L.S), and Girls Interested in Real Life Science (G.I.R.L.S.). The sites offer everything from online games to mentoring opportunities.

#62: MAKING MATH AND SCIENCE GIRL-FRIENDLY

Research indicates that as girls approach adolescence, their confidence and abilities in math and science begin to decline (AAUW, 1998; Arnow, 1995; WTN, 2000). It is at this time that math and science classes shift their focus to higher order, abstract concepts. There are several ways to mediate negative attitudes toward math and science:

1. Increase your knowledge of and enthusiasm for math and science.

2. Acknowledge the contributions of women as well as men in math and science, via posters, examples, and news articles. Invite guest speakers such as female computer scientists, accountants, and mathematicians into class.

3. Introduce lessons with big-picture concepts or an overview.

4. Provide hands-on learning opportunities in and outside of class, especially with abstract concepts. Encourage building and construction, trips to museums, and the use of chemistry sets. Assign at-home projects such as car or home repairs. In class, occasionally use shopping and cooking lessons.

5. Vary class groupings. Use whole-group problem solving and collective brainstorming. Assign partners or small groups at times, and occasionally use same-sex groupings.

6. Ask students to state concepts out loud using the vocabulary of the subject matter. Incorporate their comments into lectures or explanations to validate their knowledge.

7. In lab classes, stress safety precautions instead of emphasizing danger.

8. Use writing to help students clarify and express their feelings, such as autobiographies of mathematicians and science journals. Talk with girls about concepts.

9. Encourage risk taking. Debrief mistakes, and nurture perseverance.

10. Arrange for tutoring help. Try to find older female students.

11. Judge what girls say and not how they say it. Emphasize ability rather than luck when they achieve success.

12. Encourage girls to participate in extracurricular math and science activities. Extend a special invitation to do so.

13. Set up a Wall of Fame in the classroom to feature students' outstanding math and science work.

14. Relate what is learned in class to careers such as science and engineering.

#63: EXPLORING NEW ROLES AT SCHOOL

It is important for female and male students to pursue new experiences at school to avoid unnecessary constraints on their development as human beings. The suggestions below move students beyond gender bias at school.

Tutoring Younger Students

Older students can tutor younger students. In some cases, "near peer" relationships foster greater achievement than adult role models, due to the powerful support community that develops among students.

Girl Examples
Once girls learn word-processing, graphics, Internet use, and multimedia production, they can teach similar skills to younger students.

Boy Examples
Older boys who are successful readers and writers can tutor younger students who struggle.

Increasing Participation in the Curriculum

Both female and male students should be encouraged to participate in non-gender-specific ways at school.

Girl Examples
Girls can participate in the trio of core science classes: physics, biology, and chemistry, as well as in algebra, geometry, calculus, advanced computer science, athletics, and extracurricular activities in nontraditional areas.

They also benefit from leadership programs and participation in advanced placement courses.

Boy Examples
Boys can participate in school governance, computer buddy programs, peer mediation, conflict resolution, the arts, leadership, and newspaper and journalism classes to improve their reading and writing skills.
They also benefit from groupings that are stigma-free for basic-skills instruction.

Receiving Mentoring From Positive Role Models

Role modeling is central to learning. Students learn less from what adults say and more by what we do. It's important for all students to see women doing math and science and men involved in writing and care taking.

Girl Examples	*Boy Examples*
Girls can learn about nontraditional career choices from women engineers, mechanics, computer programmers, and economists, as well as learn about coping skills, healthy lifestyles, and personal finance.	Community members can stress the importance of good work and study skills, health, anger management, and career options in writing, the arts, or education.

#64: PEER SUPPORT NETWORKS

Often, female and male students will willingly participate in supportive and leadership roles if given opportunities to do so. Peer support networks are structured approaches to increasing academic achievement and fostering positive social relationships. The networks can be coed or same-sex and are led by teachers or community volunteers. The steps for creating such networks follow.

1. Identify a teacher or community member to oversee a peer network. Also identify a group of students who agree to participate in the network by meeting once weekly and calling their partner three times a week for one month.

2. At the first session, ask students to list what they consider to be their academic and social strengths on sheets of paper that are to be distributed as resources to other network members. Any student can freely call any other member of the network for assistance.

3. Also during the first session, ask students to identify academic or social challenges they would like to address. The challenges are turned in to the network leader.

4. Before the next meeting, the network leader reviews the students' challenges and creates pairs to work together for the next month. Ideally, each student has both a strength and challenge to engage during the upcoming month.

5. At the second session, the network leader announces pairs of students to work together. Plans are also made to meet as a group once weekly before or after school or during lunch. The students must also call their partners three times weekly for a month.

6. Partners are responsible for making lists of the assignments and social efforts they undertake as a pair. During their phone calls, they troubleshoot problems and determine whether positive strides are being made.

7. At the weekly meetings, the networkers discuss and refine their support systems.

8. At the end of the month, any individual progress should be specified, ongoing efforts identified, and the contributions made by all participants acknowledged. Most networks work best on a short-term basis. For that reason, it is good to close the network formally after one month.

#65: GENDER EQUITY BOOKMARK

Figure 3.1 is a bookmark for easy referencing in the classroom.

Figure 3.1 Gender Equity Bookmark

1. Discuss equity issues with students. Ask them to think critically to find gender bias at school and beyond.

2. In the classroom, display positive images of both genders in a variety of roles.

3. Supplement curricular resources as needed to achieve gender equity.

4. Arrange class seating charts to mix genders and, as the teacher, move about the room to be accessible to all.

5. Identify sexist language and replace it with alternate terms.

6. Be a role model of participation in a variety of activities. For example, if you are a male teacher, talk about sewing or cooking; or, if female, talk about working with tools or playing sports.

7. Notice which students are usually responded to first in discussions and why. Modify any patterns of gender bias.

8. Ask equally challenging questions of female and male students.

9. Use cooperative and competitive learning techniques.

10. Vary instructional strategies.

11. Invite guest speakers into the classroom whose skills break stereotypic gender boundaries.

12. Encourage students to consider nontraditional curricular and career choices.

SUGGESTED READINGS
FOR FURTHER INFORMATION

American Association of University Women Educational Foundation (AAUW). (1998). *Gender Gaps: Where Schools Still Fail Our Children.* Washington, DC: Author.

This report identifies the mixed progress of K-12 schools toward gender equity during the 1990s. It highlights the gains girls have made in their achievement and specifies where both sexes lag academically. Data are offered on math, science, and technology student enrollments; standardized-test score results; at-risk student issues; work force readiness, and preservice teacher education. Pointing out that new gender gaps are emerging, as in computer science, the report recommends that policymakers, testing organizations, states, school districts, teachers, and researchers take action to ensure equitable achievement opportunity. This report will appeal to those readers who want a broad overview of contemporary gender equity issues, especially as they apply to female students.

Arnow, J. (1995). *Teaching Peace: How to Raise Children to Live in Harmony Without Fear, Without Prejudice and Without Violence.* Retrieved from Worldwide Alternatives to Violence, August 3, 2002, from wwwave.org/TeachingPeace/TeachingPeaceIntro. htm

This book, generously featured in its entirety online for free, is an excellent resource for teachers confronting violence and discrimination in their schools. Chapter 4 addresses numerous aspects of gender equity including socialization processes; school-based bias concerns; discriminatory practices in math, science, and technology classrooms; teacher behaviors; and the impact of gender bias on boys. Arnow offers several suggestions for concrete action in the classroom to reduce the effects of gender bias on all students.

Education Review Office. (2000). *Promoting Boys' Achievement.* Retrieved August 3, 2002, from www.ero.govt.nz/Publications/pubs2000/promoting%20boys%20 achmt

This online report analyzes the efforts of 416 New Zealand schools to address underachievement among male students. Schools that were effective in meeting the learning needs of boys acknowledged that boys and girls learn differently and that the needs of both genders deserved attention. Efforts to address male-student underachievement included intensive reading instruction, active-learning opportunities, the inclusion of community role models, and well-articulated behavior expectations. This report revealed that at least half the schools surveyed in New Zealand were aware of the special needs of male students.

REFERENCES

American Association of University Women Educational Foundation. (1992). *How schools shortchange girls.* New York: Marlowe.

American Association of University Women Educational Foundation. (1998). *Gender gaps: Where schools still fail our children.* Washington, DC: Author.

Arnow, J. (1995). *Teaching peace: How to raise children to live in harmony without fear, without prejudice and without violence.* New York: Berkley. Retrieved August 2, 2002, from wwwave.org/TeachingPeace/TeachingPeaceIntro.htm

Aronson, E., Blaney, N., Stephan, C., Sikes, J., & Snapp, J. (1978). *The jigsaw classroom.* Beverly Hills, CA: Sage.

Bazler, J., & Simons, D. (1990). Are women out of the picture? *Science Teacher, 57*(9), 24-26.

Brown, L. M., & Gilligan, C. (1992). *Meeting at the crossroads: Women's psychology and girls' development.* Cambridge, MA: Harvard University Press.

Bullock, L. D. (1997). Efficacy of gender and ethnic equity in science education curriculum for preservice teachers. *Journal of Research in Science Teaching, 34*(10), 1019-1038.

Campbell, P. B., & Sanders, J. (1997). Uninformed but interested: Findings of a national survey on gender equity in preservice teacher education. *Journal of Teacher Education, 48*(1), 69-75.

Devon County Council (UK). (2000). *Raising boys' achievement.* Retrieved August 3, 2002, from, www.devon.gov.uk/dcs/a/boys

Educational Development Corporation. (1999). *Women's Educational Equity Act: 1999 fact sheet on women's and girls' educational equity.* Newton, MA: Author.

Education Review Office. (2000). Promoting boys' achievement. Retrieved August 2, 2002, from www.ero.govt.nz/Publications/pubs2000/promoting%20boys%20 achmt

Gay, G. (1989). Ethnic minorities and educational equality. In J. A. Banks & C. A. M. Banks (Eds.), *Multicultural education: Issues and perspectives* (pp. 167-188). Needham Heights, MA: Allyn & Bacon.

Gilligan, C. (1982). *In a different voice: Psychological theory and women's development.* Cambridge, MA: Harvard University Press.

Goldstein, G., Haldane, D., & Mitchell, C. (1990). Sex differences in visual-spatial ability: The role of performance factors. *Memory and Cognition, 18*, 546-550.

Gurian, M., Henley, P., and Trueman, T. (2001). *Boys and girls learn differently!* San Francisco: Jossey-Bass.

Haggerty, S. (1991). Gender and school science: Achievement and participation in Canada. *Alberta Journal of Educational Research, 3*, 195-208.

Hulme, M. A. (1988). Mirror, mirror on the wall: Biased reflections in textbooks and instructional materials. In A. O'B. Carellie (Ed.), *Sex equity in education* (pp. 187-206). Springfield, IL: Charles C. Thomas.

Kindlon, D., & Thompson, M. (1999). *Raising Cain: Protecting the emotional life of boys.* New York: Ballantine.

Mid-Atlantic Equity Center. (1993). *Beyond Title IX: Gender equity issues in schools.* Chevy Chase, MD: Author.

Mid-Atlantic Equity Center. (1999). *Adolescent boys: Statistics and trends* [fact sheet]. Chevy Chase, MD: Author.

Sadker, M., & Sadker, D. (1994). *Failing at fairness: How our schools cheat girls.* New York: Touchstone.

Sadker, D., & Sadker, M. (2001). Gender bias: From colonial America to today's classrooms. In J. Banks and C. Banks (Eds.), *Multicultural education: Issues and perspectives.* New York: John Wiley.

Slavin, R. (1990). *Cooperative learning.* Englewood Cliffs, NJ: Prentice Hall.

Sommers, C. H. (2000). *The war against boys.* New York: Simon & Schuster.

Tovey, R. (1995, July/August). A narrowly gender-based model of learning may end up cheating all students. *Harvard Education Letter, IX,* 3-6.

Women's Television Network Foundation. (2000). *Giving girls a foothold in the future of technology.* Retrieved August 3, 2002, from www.wnetwork.com/foundation/lessons/GIRLSTECH.PDF

Woodward, A., & Elliot, D. (1990). Textbook use and teacher professionalism. In D. Elliot & A. Woodward (Eds.), *Textbooks and schooling in the United States* (89th Yearbook of the National Society for the Study of Education, pp. 178-193). Chicago: University of Chicago Press.

Teaching Diverse Students

Addressing Language, Class, Culture, and Ability Differences in the Classroom

THE DIVERSITY OF THE U.S. EDUCATIONAL SYSTEM

The United States educational system is vast and diverse. During the 1999 to 2000 school year, the U.S. Department of Education (2001A, National Center for Educational Statistics, 2000) reported that nearly 47 million K-12 students attended our nation's public schools. Of these, 26 million were in Grades PreK-6, another 20 million were in Grades 7 to 12, and nearly 1 million attended ungraded programs. The 47 million students were housed in 92,000 schools located in 15,000 districts and taught by 2.9 million teachers.

In 2000, America's 92,000 schools were configured in numerous ways (U.S. Department of Education, 2001a). The formats consisted primarily of regular, alternative, charter, magnet, Title I, special education, and vocational schools, with considerable variation in size. Whether a school is large or small, alternative or regular, elementary or secondary, rural or urban, a commonly shared purpose is to ensure that all students gain the knowledge, skills, and information to contribute successfully to their communities throughout their lives. This national goal, while easy to state, is challenging to achieve. Regular classroom teachers endeavor to accommodate a growing student population with multiple languages, unique backgrounds and family lives, and varying academic abilities and interests. Just exactly how diverse is our country's K-12 population?

THE DIVERSITY OF K-12 STUDENTS IN THE UNITED STATES

The U.S. Department of Education (National Center for Educational Statistics, 2000), U.S. Census Bureau (2001), National Clearinghouse for English Language Acquisition (2002), and National Center for Children in Poverty (2001) track four significant categories of student diversity that we address in this chapter: (a) racial, (b) academic, (c) socioeconomic, and (d) language diversity. Though these terms may appear self-evident, there is often considerable confusion about what such concepts actually mean. As a result, federal definitions are provided for each of the four concepts below—as well as for other data of interest to administrators and teachers.

DEFINING RACIAL DIVERSITY

Since 1977, the federal government has used five categories to collect racial data (U. S. Department of Education, 1998). These categories consist of American Indian or Alaskan Native, Asian or Pacific Islander, black, white, and Hispanic. Since the late 1970s, however, the nation's population has grown more diverse, immigration has reached historic levels, and interracial marriages have increased. New terms such as biracial, multiracial, mixed heritage, and others have been suggested as additional racial categories.

DEFINING THE CONCEPT OF STUDENTS WITH DISABILITIES

Students with disabilities are those who have individualized education plans (IEPs) as required by the federal Individuals With Disabilities Education Act (IDEA) Amendments (1997), originally the Education for All Handicapped Children Act (1975). IDEA has specified multiple classifications of disability. They include mental retardation or developmental delays; learning problems; behavior or emotional disorders; communication disorders; hearing, speech, or language impairments; visual, physical and other health impairments; severe and multiple disabilities; autism; and traumatic brain injury (U.S. Department of Education, Office of Special Education and Rehabilitative Services, 2000).

The number of students with disabilities receiving special education services has grown steadily since a national count began in 1976. From 1990 to 2000, the number of special-needs students jumped 30%, a rate that was faster than both school enrollment and population growth (U.S. Department of Education, Office of Special Education and Rehabilitative Services, 2000). This increase to nearly 6,000,000 students as of 2000 has been attributed to better diagnosis and classification. Slightly over half, or 51%, of the students with disabilities were classified as having learning disabilities. The three other most prevalent forms of disability included speech and language impairments (19%), mental retardation (11%), and emotional disturbances (8%).

The 1998 to 1999 school year was the first time that the states were required to report the race and ethnicity of students served under IDEA. As a result, it was determined that white and Asian students were underrepresented in the special-education population while blacks and American Indian students were overrepresented. Hispanic students were represented at a rate comparable to the population.

DEFINING STUDENTS IN POVERTY

The National Center for Children in Poverty (2001) reported that children are more likely to live in poverty than any other age group in America and that their numbers have increased since 1979. In 1999, the federal poverty line for a family of three was $13,290 of annual income, and at that time, approximately 17% of American school-aged children lived in or near poverty. Seven percent fared worse by living in *extreme poverty*, the term used for a family of three in 1999 that earned $6,145 or less annually. Research has shown that extreme poverty during the first 5 years of life has greater negative effects for future life opportunities than extreme poverty later in childhood. Approximately 33% of minority students and 10% of white students attending school were impoverished, rates that the National Center for Children in Poverty (2001) claimed were two to three times greater than that for children in other industrialized countries.

The category of impoverished children also encompasses those who are homeless. The Stewart B. McKinney Homeless Assistance Act of 1987 (Legal Information Institute, Cornell University, n. d.) federally defined the homeless as individuals who lack fixed, regular, or adequate residences. A fixed residence is permanent and unchanging. A regular residence is used consistently, and an adequate one meets the psychological and physical needs of a home. Examples of homeless students include those in emergency, runaway, or transitional shelters; those living in deserted buildings or on the streets; those staying temporarily in camping grounds or trailer parks; those waiting for permanent placement by state agencies; or those abandoned by their families. While only estimates are available of the number of homeless adults and children, the U.S. Department of Education reported that approximately 700,000 K-12 students were homeless during 1998 (National Center for Homeless Education, n.d.). Though assumed to be an urban problem, approximately one third of the homeless are in rural areas (Vissing, 1996). As might be expected, due, in part, to the irregularity of their attendance, many homeless students encounter significant educational challenges.

DEFINING LIMITED ENGLISH PROFICIENT STUDENTS

Limited English proficient (LEP) students, also referred to as language minority students or English language learners (ELL), are those living in households where a language other than English is the primary language. Language minority students are the fastest growing population in U.S. schools, and they represent a broad spectrum of language proficiency (Ovando & Collier, 1998). Such students range from indigenous minorities whose ancestors have lived in North America for tens of thousands of years to recent immigrants from countries around the world.

Title VII of the Improving America's Schools Act (1994) legally defines Limited English proficient (LEP) students. According to Title VII, an LEP student is a child who "has sufficient difficulty speaking, reading, writing, or understanding the English language and whose difficulties may deny such individual the opportunity to learn successfully in classrooms where the language of instruction is English or to participate fully in our society" (Sec. 7501). As such, they are entitled to identification and placement services. Services may include bilingual or English as a Second Language (ESL) programs. To distinguish between these two services, bilingual programs provide some native-language content instruction while students also learn English during part of the school day. In ESL programs, students receive content instruction in English and are pulled out of the classroom for part of the day to learn English skills with other LEP students. The U.S. Department of Education (2001b) reported that ESL programs were more common than bilingual programs, and that 13% of schools enrolling LEP students have neither program. It should be noted that while the term LEP is used extensively in literature and demographic data, some prefer the use of ELL, since it avoids connoting deficiency until full English proficiency is attained (Ovando & Collier, 1998).

During the decade from 1990 to 2000, the National Clearinghouse for English Language Acquisition (2002) reported that the numbers of LEP students have more than doubled from 2 million in 1990 to over 4 million in 2000. As of 2000, about three fourths of the students spoke Spanish; the nine other largest groups, in descending order, were Vietnamese, Hmong, Cantonese, Cambodian, Korean, Laotian, Navaho, Tagalog, and Russian. Demographic projections indicate that language diversity among K-12 students will continue to increase. A summary of data is displayed in Table 4.1.

IMPLICATIONS OF STUDENT DIVERSITY FOR THE CLASSROOM

All K-12 students are entitled to access, equity, and quality academic experiences. Equitable education can be best accomplished through inclusive classrooms that acknowledge and respond to student differences. Inclusive classrooms underscore a fundamental truth about any group of students: that not everyone functions at an equivalent level in all subjects. They also prevent

Table 4.1   K-12 Student Diversity in the United States

Category	Approximate K-12 Student Numbers Based on 47,000,000	Approximate Percentage of K-12 Student Population
Racial Diversity		
Among Students		
American Indian and Alaska Natives	500,000	1%
Asian and Pacific Islanders	2,000,000	4%
Hispanics	7,000,000	16%
Blacks	8,000,000	17%
Whites	29,000,000	62%
Students With Disabilities:		
All K-12 students	6,000,000	12%
Students in Poverty:		
All K-12 students	8,000,000	17%
Homeless K-12 students	700,000	1%
Limited English Proficient Students		
All K-12 students	4,000,000	8%

social stratification, an important educational goal (Hallahan & Kauffman, 1994; Oakes, 1985; Page, 1991; Slavin, 1987; Wheelock, 1992).

Fortunately, there is a body of literature that can be relied on for the effective instruction of a wide array of students. The teaching practices that I describe in this chapter fall under the broad umbrella of inclusive instruction. In this chapter, I summarize some of what has been learned about teaching approaches that result in positive achievement gains for diverse students. And I give examples of instructional techniques that target specific groups of students, such as LEP or special needs. In practice, however, the majority of strategies can be used in most classrooms.

TEACHING SPECIAL NEEDS STUDENTS IN MAINSTREAM CLASSROOMS

Teacher attitudes and attributes have proven to be an important predictor for the achievement of special needs students (Baum, Renzulli, & Hebert, 1995; Coates, 1989; Idol, Nevin, & Paolucci-Whitcomb, 1994; Olson, Chalmers, & Hoover, 1997). Teachers who are skilled at integrating special needs students in the classroom have been found to be tolerant, reflective, and flexible. They accept responsibility for all students and demonstrate warmth and acceptance in their interactions.

Multilevel instruction, sometimes referred to as differentiated instruction, is a strategy in which the teacher prepares one lesson with variations for individual students. Tutoring has proven effective in raising achievement among learning-disabled and other students who are behind in grade level skills (Elbaum, Moody, Vaughn, Schumm, & Hughes, 1999; Gersten, Baker, Marks, & Smith, 1999; Schumm, Vaughn, & Sobol, 1997; U.S. Department of Education, 1997a). In this chapter, I describe techniques for multilevel instruction, the monitoring of student understanding, and tutoring practices to benefit special needs and, ultimately, all students.

Effective, inclusive teachers also target reading as an essential skill and work to ensure strong literacy achievement of all students. For example, one research study showed that a daily reading course included in an urban multiethnic high school curriculum yielded reading achievement gains four times those of those students not taking the course (Allington, 2001).

Inclusive teachers also consider ways to meet the needs of gifted students in the classroom. Since there are no federal guidelines for defining gifted students, the identification of such students is locally determined by schools, districts and, in some cases, at the state level. Gifted children can be found in all racial, language, and socioeconomic groups and they tend to share some or all of the following characteristics: they learn quickly, are highly motivated, have excellent memories, perceive relationships, and may demonstrate advanced skills or knowledge of a discipline (Frasier & Passow, 1994; Subotnik & LeBlanc, 2001). Gifted students benefit from instruction that accommodates their intense curiosity. I suggest ways to nurture their talents within the regular classroom.

INTEGRATING LIMITED ENGLISH PROFICIENT STUDENTS INTO MAINSTREAM CLASSROOMS

Not enough teachers have been trained to work with language minority students. As a result, educators are left to improvise and seek out professional development. Fortunately, recent research has identified effective approaches that monolingual, mainstream teachers can use in their classrooms. To begin, teachers can modulate their use of English to improve the comprehension of those who are learning our language (Brice & Roseberry-McKibbin, 1999; Gersten et al., 1999). Additionally, a 14-year study from 1982 to 1996 of 700,000 language minority student records in five school districts revealed methods that promoted the strong achievement of ELLs (Thomas & Collier, 1997). These included collaborative, interactive, interdisciplinary, and discovery approaches to learning. Some examples are described later in this chapter.

Another group of ELL students who deserve special attention are those who may be preliterate due to a lack of opportunity either to attend school in their former countries or to learn how to read and write in their native languages. Strategies for meeting the needs of these special students are also addressed in this chapter.

TEACHING RACIALLY DIVERSE STUDENTS

Over the last several years, schools and teachers have embraced multicultural education. In addition to preparing students to live in an ethnically diverse society, multicultural education also strives to balance ethnocentric traditional curriculum; enhance racial understanding; and make the curriculum responsive to the experiences, traditions, and historical and contemporary contributions of the nation's population. Additionally, many educators and researchers claim that multicultural education also leads to enhanced academic achievement (Gay, 2001; Revilla & Sweeney, 1997; Webb, 1990). In this chapter, multicultural perspectives are infused into discussions of mathematics and literature studies. Through such efforts, not only do minority students benefit but so also do majority students whose appreciation for the tapestry of American life is broadened and deepened.

There is tremendous language diversity across the United States. Numbers not only of language minority students but also of nonstandard English speakers are increasing. Many students speak black English, Appalachian English, Indian English, and Hawaiian Creole, to name a few dialects. Nonstandard English usage is also prevalent among diverse social classes (Joos, 1967; Payne, 1995). Schools and teachers can successfully teach formal English while affirming the importance of students' home dialects and encouraging them to communicate in both languages, as appropriate. Strategies addressing this issue will be found later in the chapter.

TEACHING STUDENTS IN POVERTY

While being poor does not necessarily equate with underachievement, students in poverty do bring special needs to schools. Fortunately, research on Title I schools (Diamond & Moore, 1993; Revilla & Sweeney, 1997) and Haberman's (1995) three decades of studies on "star teachers" of children of poverty reveal teacher characteristics and instructional strategies that boost the performance of disadvantaged children.

Some children in poverty move frequently. While changing schools can occasionally yield positive effects, such as taking advantage of a fresh start socially or accessing new academic programs, frequent mobility usually results in negative consequences. Students who are highly transient are at greater risk for underachievement, misbehavior, and youth violence (Educational Research Service, 2001). Mobility also adversely affects schools by slowing the pace of instruction, lowering teacher morale, and adding to administrative loads. While it is unlikely that student mobility will suddenly decrease, schools and teachers can take steps to mitigate some of its harmful effects (Arroyo, Rhoad, & Drew, 1999; Educational Research Service, 2001).

REFLECTING ON TEACHING IN DIVERSE CLASSROOMS

Perhaps more than any other phenomenon in education, the diversity of K-12 students serves as the greatest catalyst for professional growth. While U.S. teachers are predominantly white, female, and middle-class, particularly in elementary schools, our students represent an array of linguistic, racial, academic, and socioeconomic groups. The diversity in the classroom encourages us to confront our beliefs about those we teach. We can ponder questions such as, What are my assumptions about diverse groups? Where did I acquire such notions? How do these beliefs influence my attitudes toward my students and instruction? What do I need to unlearn and learn? How? The rest of this chapter puts tools into teachers' hands to work more successfully with all students in the classroom.

#66: LEVELING LESSONS

Leveling enables academically diverse students to work on similar curriculum but at levels appropriate to their abilities (see Figure 4.1). The same lesson can accommodate varying degrees of complexity and depth. Because of limited time and energy in busy teachers' schedules, leveling can be done by a teacher, a group of teachers at a grade level or in a subject, or by teachers in special workshops outside the school. It may not be possible to reformat all lessons in all situations. When leveling is appropriate, the following guidelines can guide lesson development. This information is adapted from the work of Collicott (1991, pp. 191-218).

• Consider the specific knowledge or skills to be taught. These may be based on state standards or district curriculum guidelines.

• Determine how to informally preassess students' knowledge and skills.

• Identify an instructional strategy to present the content of the lesson. Based on teaching experience, textbook recommendations, or input from colleagues, use a strategy that will effectively incorporate the specific components of the knowledge or skill being targeted.

• Visualize a range of knowledge or ability from students with minimal understanding of the content to advanced understanding. How broad or deep is their prior knowledge? How complex are their skills? Consider how your identified strategy will meet the needs of students along this continuum.

• Determine how you will modify your designated activity for various students in your class. Two versions may be enough, but depending on the range of students, it may take three or even more versions. The modifications may involve different materials, groupings, vocabulary, rates of presentation, or entry points to the lesson.

• Align each student or group of students in the class with a corresponding modification in the lesson. Make sure that each student's needs are addressed and that each student is appropriately challenged.

• Identify a meaningful and appropriate assessment activity. Since students learn at different levels, they should have the opportunity to demonstrate their learning at different levels.

Figure 4.1 Leveling Curriculum

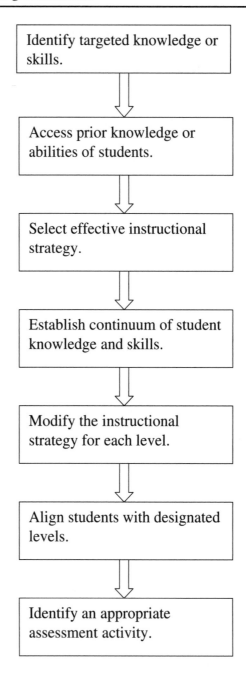

SOURCE: Adapted from J. Collicott (1991, pp. 191-218).

#67: MULTILEVEL SPELLING

The following "leveled" spelling strategy teaches one lesson while encouraging varied student experiences and responses. As such, it is appropriate for use with gifted or challenged students, the learning disabled, or ELLs. Students develop individualized spelling lists from three sources: (a) teacher generated words, (b) student-identified words from academic content, and (c) student-identified words from everyday life or their career interests. They also problem solve their own strategies for accurate spelling. This strategy is adapted from the work of Johnson (1999, p. 76).

1.   Generate and distribute a spelling list of approximately 10 to 20 words.

2.   Ask students to add to your list by identifying five or more spelling words they want to learn from diverse subject areas. Teachers may assist some students in compiling such lists.

3.   Ask students to add five or more words from their everyday lives or from their career interests. Each student should provide the teacher with an individualized list of five discipline-based words and five career or everyday spelling words.

4.   Once the spelling lists are compiled, organize students into heterogeneous groups of approximately three or four. Include one strong speller, one weak speller, and one or two average spellers in each group.

5.   While in their groups, ask students to brainstorm effective approaches to studying their spelling words. Encourage each student to contribute at least one strategy, and suggest that the groups be creative. They can use color, shape, size, and sound when working with their words; or create mnemonic devices, flash cards, or games. After their discussions, ask the groups to select a person to compile a list of each member's suggested strategies.

6.   Ask that the small groups explain or demonstrate one or more of their techniques to the class. Once the groups have shared, compile a comprehensive list of suggested spelling-word strategies, and later distribute the list to all students.

7.   When students have received the combined list of suggestions for studying spelling words, the teacher should select a few to discuss, demonstrate, and practice with the entire class.

8.   Next, ask students to select strategies to use when studying their words. Such techniques may be individualized approaches or include teacher or peer assistance.

9.   Plan to set aside some class time for students to study their spelling words. Some may work independently, with partners, or in small groups. Markers, note cards, and other resources should be available as needed.

10.   During the study session, move from student to student or group to group to support and clarify processes and to assist students in assessing their pelling improvement. Students will likely be engaged in a variety of activities during such sessions. For example, a pair may have made spelling games and be receiving feedback on their efforts. Other pairs may ask each other to orally spell selected words. Some may write paragraphs using specific words.

11.   After the study sessions, ask the class to discuss the most effective studying strategies, perhaps generating a top 5 or 10 list.

12.   Assess students' spelling skills individually through written or oral means.

#68: DO THEY GET IT? ASSESSING STUDENT UNDERSTANDING IN INCLUSIVE CLASSROOMS

As teachers know all too well, once a lesson begins, some students exhibit confusion or disengagement. Research shows that the lower the students' achievement, the more reluctant they are to reveal their lack of understanding (Nelson-LeGall, 1985). Teachers should be vigilant about checking in with students to see if they understand assignments, lectures, or homework. Several monitoring techniques are suggested in this strategy, which are appropriate for highly diverse student groups.

Ask Content and Process Questions

Asking both content and process questions can strengthen questioning during class time. Content questions ask, What is the answer? while process questions ask, How did you arrive at that answer?

Circulate Around the Room

Research shows that effective teachers move around the classroom to monitor students and their work. Such informal observations give teachers opportunities to gauge student understanding and intervene quickly as needed.

Ensure Understanding at the Beginning of an Assignment

Make sure students understand concepts and directions at the beginning of a lesson to ward off confusion and mistakes. You might ask students to rephrase your directions, summarize the steps of a task, or ask clarifying questions.

Check Student Understanding at Frequent Intervals

Ask students to summarize key points of a task at frequent intervals. This lets the teacher observe whether students are on track or need redirection.

Encourage Students to Ask Questions

Make asking questions a classroom norm. Encourage students, especially those who struggle, to ask clarifying questions. When introducing or practicing a complex concept, remind students that learning is challenging and that asking questions or requesting assistance can improve learning.

Use Feedback Forms

Distribute prepared feedback forms at the beginning of a lesson. They can include phrases such as, It was easy for me to . . . , What I learned was . . . ,

What I don't understand is . . . , I am confused about . . . , I would like to review.
. . . Students can use these forms during a lesson to record their reactions, and
hand them in at the end of a lesson.

Give Practice Tests

Before an actual test, give students a practice test to see what they have
learned. The tests should be short and brief. They can be open- or closed-book
and administered to students individually, in pairs, or in small groups. Students
can use practice tests to review what they have learned and to identify what
needs to be studied further. Feedback should be immediate.

SOURCE: "Are They Getting it? How to Monitor Student Understanding in Inclusive Classrooms" by
J. S. Schumm, S. Vaughn, & M. C. Sobol (1997, January). *Intervention in School and Clinic, 32*(3), 168-171.
Copyright by PRO-ED, Inc. Adapted with permission.

#69: TEACHING ELEMENTARY READERS

Primary-grade teachers have the enormous responsibility of teaching children to read. While some students will learn to read almost effortlessly, others require explicit and focused instruction. Research has identified approaches to preventing reading problems among young students. Some of that information is synthesized in the following checklist of 11 suggestions that teachers of Grades 1 to 3 can use to ensure the literacy achievement of all students. Check all the listed items that reflect your current efforts, and put a star by any approaches that you would like to add.

To teach reading in my classroom, I consistently:

1. ____ Teach and model letter and sound skills and spelling-sound correspondences (Pressley et al., 2001; Snow et al., 1998)

2. ____ Teach high-frequency or sight recognition words (Snow et al., 1998)

3. ____ Encourage children to write often (Snow et al., 1998)

4. ____ Support students' initial use of invented spelling and develop correct spelling through focused instruction and practice (Snow et al., 1998)

5. ____ Provide a rich literacy environment with two types of instructional materials: (a) those that students can easily read to themselves and (b) those that students can learn to read with assistance (Snow et al., 1998)

6. ____ Encourage those students who are beginning to read independently to sound out and confirm unfamiliar words rather than relying on context clues alone (Snow et al., 1998)

7. ____ Teach two or more reading skills during each hour of reading instruction, and design lessons so students spend much more time reading and writing than preparing or following up (Pressley et al., 2001)

8. ____ Explicitly teach comprehension strategies such as summarizing the main idea, predicting events and outcomes, creating mental images, drawing inferences, and monitoring for coherence and misunderstandings (Pressley et al., 2001; Snow et al., 1998)

9. ____ Teach students to plan, draft, and revise as part of the writing process (Pressley et al., 2001)

10. ____ Give students printed prompts to guide their writing process (posters, cards, or tips posted on bulletin boards that explain what to do during revision) (Pressley et al., 2001)

11. ____ Promote reading and writing outside school through daily, at-home assignments and expectations, summer activities, and inclusion of parents and others such as public librarians (Snow et al., 1998)

#70: HELPING STRUGGLING INTERMEDIATE READERS

Some children make adequate progress during the primary grades with reading but later encounter difficulties. It is professionally responsible to assume that many students will require ongoing support with literacy achievement. Strategies derived from the research of Allington (2001) and the U.S. Department of Education's National Institute for Literacy (2000) target struggling intermediate-level readers for assistance. Several classroom approaches are listed below.

1. Plan to provide struggling readers with four types of support: (a) access to books at appropriate reading and interest levels, (b) long-term support from a reading specialist or resource or development center, (c) extra support for reading in the content areas (see Activity # 73), and (d) school-family reading coordination.

2. Expand instructional time for reading. Add a second daily reading lesson taught by the classroom or specialist teacher or offer before- or after-school programs.

3. Assess students' reading ability frequently. Particularly target their comprehension and their fluency, and, when problems are noted, plan instruction or assistance accordingly.

4. Focus on enhancing vocabulary. Some students benefit when their teachers take dictation of their statements. The students read what they have said and memorize spelling and punctuation accordingly. To help students develop extensive sight vocabularies, some teachers make lists of words from age-appropriate selections they read aloud. Each student has a box of index cards and keeps adding selected words to study. Later, they use these words in narrative and expository writing.

5. Model reading and comprehension strategies for students. Post such techniques on bulletin boards or walls.

6. Vary student opportunities for reading. Ask them to read in pairs and small groups. Also ask students to read out loud by first skimming a text for answers and then reading aloud the words or phrases that provide the answers to questions posed in class.

7. Vary the types of materials students are asked to read, such as stories, reports, letters, newspapers, and Web site information.

#71: TEACHING READING IN THE CONTENT AREAS

Providing support for students in content area classes is an important component of a systemic approach to strong literacy achievement. Content area teachers do not have to forgo their subject matter to focus on reading. Instead, they can explicitly integrate reading supports into everyday instruction. When they do, students have greater opportunities to work with grade-level materials and to avoid confusion and frustration when reading text materials. Several suggestions for content area teachers follow.

1. Think about your instruction of new content as having three phases. The first activates students' background knowledge, the second constructs new knowledge, and the third asks students to apply and use the new knowledge.

2. Model and discuss your own reading processes to make them explicit for students. Perhaps you might explain that, after reading a page or two, you stop to summarize key ideas in your own words.

3. Give students a clear purpose or goal for reading.

4. Ask what students may already know about the topic and apply that knowledge to the text to be read.

5. Define key terms, interpret important phrases, and ask students to look for them when they read.

6. With students working individually at first, ask them to predict what they think the 5 or 10 most important words will be in a reading selection. Next, put students in pairs to cooperatively develop their top 5 or 10 words. Ask all students to read the material, to note the important concepts, and, in pairs, to revise their original lists.

7. Explain text features such as headings, graphs, and pictures that can help students predict the content of the text. Ask them to make and test predictions.

8. Ask students to keep a journal in which they write out definitions and explore important concepts.

9. Set aside time for reflection on what was read. Ask students to summarize main ideas in sections of text; or to make charts, outlines, or webs of the content they covered.

10. Encourage recreational reading of high-interest materials such as sports statistics for math or science fiction books for science.

#72: HELPING STRUGGLING ADOLESCENT READERS

Weak reading ability, rather than illiteracy, is a common concern of many secondary-level teachers. According to the 1998 National Assessment of Educational Progress (NAEP) (U.S. Department of Education, National Center for Educational Statistics, n.d.), about one fourth of 8th graders and one fifth of 12th graders read below the basic level. This means that they do not understand the main ideas of a text, make inferences, or relate what they have read to their personal lives. Some secondary schools are developing approaches to improving the reading achievement of their students through a reading-apprentice approach (Association for Supervision and Curriculum Development, 2000; Educational Research Service, 2001). Some apprentice activities are described below.

Reading Apprenticeships

1. Teachers serve as "master readers" and work with students who are "apprentice readers" to analyze the reading process and teach how to read nonliterary texts.

2. Students are taught metacognitive skills to identify what they do and don't understand when confronted with a variety of texts.

3. Together, students and teachers sometimes work their way through a reading selection and use reciprocal-teaching techniques. These include predicting, clarifying, questioning, and summarizing. To clarify what they have read, for example, students might reread portions of the text or discuss them in small groups, then read further in the text to see if the meaning becomes clear, or connect what they are reading with their lives.

4. The teacher asks students to examine 10 or more unidentified text excerpts. These might include selections taken from a job application, a tax form, a magazine quiz, academic texts, directions for assembling a computer, or samples of commercial writing. Students are asked to categorize each selection, identify its use, and rate their understanding of each item. They then must decide which reading skills to use to improve their understanding of the difficult texts.

5. Twice weekly, students engage in sustained silent reading with self-selected materials. Some of this reading will be in school, and some will be outside school hours—in a reading club after school or at home. They must maintain weekly reading logs, read 200 pages a month, and do monthly culminating projects in which they reflect on themselves as readers.

#73: USING TUTORS TO INCREASE READING ACHIEVEMENT

Well-designed tutoring programs that use volunteers and nonprofessionals as tutors can significantly raise students' reading achievement (Educational Research Service, 2001; U.S. Department of Education, 1997a). Research consistently shows that several forms of tutoring, whether peer, cross-age, or adult tutoring, can improve the reading achievement of the disadvantaged, mildly disabled, and ELLs. Teachers or schools wanting to implement effective tutoring options for their remedial readers, can choose from among the models of effective programs listed below.

Connect Tutoring Content With Classroom Reading Instruction

Students perform better when tutors align their efforts with good classroom-reading practices. The tutoring should be in line with classroom instruction. Structured sessions that contain opportunities for rereading classroom materials, analyzing words, and allowing writing opportunities are beneficial.

Provide Tutors With Ongoing Training

Tutors who receive training and feedback throughout their participation attain better results with students than those who do not receive such coaching. Important topics to cover with tutors include tips for establishing positive interpersonal relationships with students, strategies for reinforcing correct responses and correcting mistakes, ways to structure the tutoring sessions, and how to model reading and writing processes. Reading specialists might provide such training and oversight.

Offer Frequent Tutoring Sessions

Successful tutoring programs run from 10 to 30 minutes and pair the same tutor and tutee three times weekly. This frequency of sessions generates greater achievement than tutoring that is scheduled twice weekly or less.

Use a Variety of Tutors

Studies have shown that a wide variety of people can effectively serve as tutors. Peer or cross-age tutors can effectively improve reading skills of their tutees. Even at-risk, middle school, LEP students have successfully tutored low-achieving elementary students and improved their own skills in the process. College students, paraprofessionals, retirees, volunteers, and parents can all work effectively as tutors with support and oversight.

Design Interventions
for Students With Disabilities

Trained volunteers with careful supervision from reading or resource teachers can successfully work with students with severe reading difficulties. In such cases, a certified reading specialist can assess children's reading skills and needs, develop lesson plans, observe tutors, and provide them with feedback. Important strategies for improving reading and learning among struggling readers include instilling an appreciation of written material, printed language, and the writing system; teaching the alphabet; developing students' phonological skills and phonemic awareness; teaching phonics, spelling, and vocabulary skills; and fluency and reflective reading.

Provide Ongoing
Assessment of Tutored Students

Frequently assess students' reading skills so that tutoring can be tailored to meet their individual needs.

#74: AN EXTRA NET: USING WEB SITES TO SUPPORT THE NEEDS OF DIVERSE LEARNERS

There is a growing number of educationally sound Web sites available on the Internet. The sites listed below are maintained by credible organizations and offer content that matches common curricular goals. Their content provides both practice and enrichment for a variety of students. Make certain, however, before students access the Internet at school, that your building has an Acceptable Use Policy in place and that parents or caregivers have given written permission for their children to use the Internet.

Mathematics

- Algebra for Grades 8 to12
  www.algebra-online.com/ (retrieved August 9, 2002).

Students can ask questions and receive assistance for free.

- Everyday math for Grades K-12
  www.learner.org/exhibits/dailymath/ (retrieved August 9, 2002).

Students learn how math skills are used in everyday life.

- GirlTECH math for Grades 3 to 11
  www.crpc.rice.edu/CRPC/Women/GirlTECH/Lessons/ (retrieved August 9, 2002).

Challenging and enriching math content is presented for girls.

- Multiplication facts for Grades 3 to 7
  www.thinkquest.org/library/lib/site_sum_outside.html?tname=3896&cid=2&url=3896/index2.htm (retrieved August 9, 2002).

This site provides helpful assistance for students learning multiplication.

Language Arts

- Li'l Fingers for Toddlers to Preschoolers
  www.lil-fingers.com/storybooks/index.html (retrieved August 9, 2002).

This Web site encourages young children to read engaging stories with words, pictures, and some technological flair.

- Reading motivators for Grades 2 to 6
  kids.MysteryNet.com/ (retrieved August 9, 2002).

For the reluctant reader, this site is filled with engaging activities, such as scary stories, contests, and mysteries to solve.

- Oral presentations for Grades 2 to 12
  www.ukans.edu/cwis/units/coms2/virtualassistants.html (retrieved August 9, 2002).

Students receive assistance in improving their public speaking skills.

- Publishing student work online for Grades K-12
  www.kidstuff.org/ (retrieved August 9, 2002);
  www.english.unitecnology.ac.nz/writers/home.html (retrieved August 9, 2002).

These two sites encourage students to publish their written work and to read the work of their peers.

- Vocabulary development for Grades 4 to 12
  www.vocabulary.com (retrieved August 9, 2002)

Vocabulary is taught through thematic puzzles at three levels of difficulty.

- Writing conventions for Grades 3 to 12
  webster.commnet.edu/grammar/(retrieved August 9, 2002)

Students can practice numerous aspects of writing conventions including grammar, sentence structure, and the principles of writing effective compositions.

#75: ENGAGING THE GIFTED

Gifted students often learn more quickly than their peers and want to explore content in greater depth and complexity. Here are 10 techniques to help them jump ahead.

1. With the whole class, brainstorm a list of independent choices students can make when they have successfully completed their work. Post the list in the classroom and encourage students to select one or two activities to pursue when appropriate.

2. Encourage those who have finished work ahead of their peers to pursue additional reading, help other classmates, or go to the library for independent study. Have students who pursue independent reading keep reading logs to hand in for review. Such a log might look like Figure 4.2.

3. Set aside blocks of time in the classroom or library for students to pursue projects and discussions.

4. Secure permission from other teachers for your students to attend their classes as a way to enrich their learning.

5. Accelerate the pace of study in your classroom for gifted students by allowing them to complete assignments at a faster pace.

6. If assignments appear too easy for some students, allow them to demonstrate mastery of the content without extensive practice and drill, and then move on.

7. Extend content by asking students to consider multiple perspectives, current events, or historical components to deepen their knowledge base.

8. Identify an older student or adult mentor to supervise a highly capable student's self-selected project.

9. Occasionally group gifted students together to collaborate on assignments.

10. Identify broad concepts such as power, conflict, or beauty and ask students to extend the regular curriculum by thematically considering added dimensions of their studies.

Figure 4.2 Reading Log

Date	Title and Author	Pages: from ___ to ___	Responses: I wonder, predict, question, think, was reminded of, am curious about:

#76: HELPING NEW AND INCOMING STUDENTS

Going to a new school can be a stressful experience for students and their families as well as for the classroom teachers. Schools can establish procedures to welcome and engage new students while easing the transition of their relocation, as in the procedures described below and adapted (except for the second #6) from the Educational Research Service (2001, p. 9).

Before a New Student Arrives

1. Have orientation packets to distribute that feature school and teacher profiles, a student handbook, news articles or school newsletters, yearbooks, extracurricular information, and important contact numbers.

2. Establish a newcomers club to meet once weekly with counselors or others.

3. Administer short basic-skill assessments to identify where a student might best be placed.

4. Maintain packets of core readings or assignments to give to incoming students to orient them to classrooms.

5. Create referral procedures.

6. Plan and host an orientation or open house exclusively for new students and their families. Nearly all students in one study said they appreciated meeting a school staff member before attending classes (Jalongo, 1994).

7. Enlist students' assistance in orienting new classmates to the school.

8. Create a short list of school and classroom procedures.

Ongoing Procedures

1. Explicitly model and explain classroom routines and expectations.

2. Use collaborative learning in the classroom, and foster positive peer interactions.

3. Individualize instruction as needed and provide tutoring or enrichment before or after school or during lunch.

4. Address the students' physical and psychosocial needs, and link them with appropriate resources.

5. Articulate student strengths. Communicate high expectations.

6. Encourage goal-setting and age-appropriate self-determination. Celebrate accomplishments.

7. Contact the parents or caregivers to welcome them to the school and to inform them about classrooms and programs.

8. Offer independent study options for new students to make up missed credits.

9. Maintain portfolios and work samples to document academic growth.

10. Have teachers or students invite newcomers to participate in the school's extracurricular programs.

SOURCE: Adapted from Educational Research Service (2001, p. 9).

#77: MEETING THE NEEDS
OF PRELITERATE ENGLISH
LANGUAGE LEARNER STUDENTS

Immigrant or refugee students are appearing in greater numbers in the schools. Some, who have left war-torn countries or suffered catastrophic natural disasters, may not have attended school regularly if at all. As a result, some ELLs may be preliterate and require specialized support. Ten suggestions for improving the achievement of preliterate students are listed below. They are adapted from the work of the Northwest Regional Educational Laboratory (2001).

1. To increase cultural awareness and sensitivity, teachers should learn about the values, traditions, and customs of the students in their classes. This can be accomplished through reading, conducting Internet searches, attending classes, participating in immigrant community events, and having conversations with members of a particular group. Once learned, knowledge of a student's home culture can be integrated into instruction by using culturally familiar examples or topics.

2. Learn about varied immigrant experiences and use such information background knowledge as appropriate to tap in the classroom. One caveat, however, is to consider the fears of undocumented students. Additionally, teachers may want to know their district and state polices regarding information about students' and families' immigration status.

3. Encourage parents or others to read with students in their native languages. Regardless of the language, knowledge of text structure, rhetorical devices, visual-perceptual skills, and cognitive processes transfer from one language to another.

4. Provide one-on-one literacy instruction in the native and English languages. Research shows the best long-term achievement gains occur when students become literate in their primary language first (Ovando & Collier, 1998). Likewise, reading skills can be developed in both languages simultaneously with no negative academic consequences. Teacher aides, student teachers, and volunteers may offer individualized tutoring sessions. Providing personalized attention to older students can help close the achievement gap and prevent them from dropping out of school altogether.

5. Establish a positive and supportive environment that encourages all students to engage in conversational opportunities in the classroom. At the same time, be aware that ELL students may experience a nonverbal or silent period as they develop new language skills and confidence in new settings.

6.   Make an effort to learn some vocabulary in the native language of students to better communicate with them. If able, learn key words or phrases to integrate into the instruction of key concepts or skills.

7.   Increase students' ability to understand English by selecting familiar topics of conversation, creating a context (see activities in Chapter 1) for what is to be learned, using simple sentence constructions, repeating important phrases, and matching your body language to what you are stating.

8.   Enlist the assistance of a school's ESL teacher to provide classes that target cognitive and academic development, oral-language skills, and practice in reading and writing.

9.   Encourage your school to offer programs or refer students to programs that extend beyond academics. These might include counseling services that are sensitive to the students' backgrounds, health referrals to meet the physical needs of students and their families, communicating with parents in their own languages, and offering extracurricular and career guidance programs to help students succeed in school and in their communities.

10.   Research and develop a newcomer program to help orient immigrant students and their families to the school and its programs.

SOURCE: Adapted from Northwest Regional Educational Laboratory (2001).

#78: USING ENGLISH EFFECTIVELY WITH ENGLISH LANGUAGE LEARNERS

In classrooms of all English-speaking students, common norms of schooling, such as questions, lectures, and oral directions and feedback prevail. However, such practices can be rethought when ELLs are present. There are simple techniques that mainstream teachers can integrate into daily instruction to increase the comprehension of language minority students.

Before Instruction

- Teach essential instruction and vocabulary words before assigning a task.
- Focus on 5 to 10 core vocabulary words in each lesson.
- Sit students from similar cultural and linguistic groups together for peer support.
- If possible, have instructions translated into students' native languages and written on cards for them to refer to during the assignment.
- If possible, have visual images with English labels of the steps of the assignment or task.

Giving Instructions for Assignments

- Speak slowly and pause frequently.
- Avoid run-on sentences.
- Use butcher paper or an overhead projector to clarify oral directions.
- Use idiom-free language since not all students will understand expressions such as, "We had to twist her arm to participate."
- Emphasize key words in your speech, such as, "Get your *paper* and *pencils*. Turn to *page 54* in your *textbooks*. We will solve problems *one through five* on *page 54.*"

During an Assignment

- Use small-group activities to decrease isolation and increase participation.
- Use multimodal teaching processes as described in Chapter 2.
- Use visuals.
- Have one or more other students model doing the assignment first.
- Relate content to students' background cultural knowledge as much as possible. For example, the teacher can compare food, climate, clothing, holidays, or jobs of various locations.

- Increase wait time when asking a question.
- Ask only one question at a time.
- Avoid gestures, such as pointing, that may be considered culturally inappropriate.

At the End of an Assignment

- Ask for a brief oral or written summary of what was learned.
- Ask for opinions about the assignment.
- Have students show what was completed.
- Determine whether students met the instructional goals. If not, plan for tutoring or additional practice; or seek the services of a school or district ESL specialist.

#79: GEOMETRIC COLLABORATION

The strategic use of resources, limited language, peer learning, and charting can effectively introduce students to geometric concepts. To begin, organize students into pairs or small groups. Provide each group with textbooks, encyclopedias, or other materials that address the following common geometric figures. Adapt, copy, and distribute the form in Figure 4.3A.

Figure 4.3A   Geometric Shapes

Vocabulary	Written Definition	Drawing	Classroom Example
Line			
Ray			
Point			
Circle			
Degree			
Diameter			
Radius			
Arc			

Other terms for geometric figures can be added. Additionally, the figure can be adapted to include formulas for finding volume, perimeter, and circumference (see Figure 4.3B).

Figure 4.3B Geometric Figures

Vocabulary	What is it?	What does it look like?	How do you find it?
Cube			
Cylinder			
Pyramid			
Rectangular prism			
Triangular prism			

#80: COLLABORATIVE NOTE TAKING

Students' class notes often reveal what they learned and did not learn during a lesson. For some students, note taking is distracting and confusing and, ultimately, unhelpful in preparing for tests. Such skills, however, can be improved when practiced collaboratively.

Ask your class to take notes during a lecture. For early grades—perhaps Grades 3, 4, and 5—the lecture should be brief (under 6 minutes) and clearly structured. Afterward, divide students into small, collaborative groups. Provide time for the groups to discuss the lecture and to identify its key points and important examples or supporting details. After their discussions, ask students to add new information to their notes. Next, ask questions of the small groups, and let them respond with a collective response. Later encourage all students to use their collaborative notes for studying for tests or other class assignments (Schumm, Vaughn, & Sobel, 1997, p. 170).

#81: TEACHING STANDARD ENGLISH IN THE MULTICULTURAL CLASSROOM

Many students speak dialects that differ from standard English. In the classroom, nonstandard English speakers should be encouraged to retain the language of their home, community, and peers while at the same time acquiring the language of education. Teachers can teach standard English with cultural sensitivity and ensure that students are successful with both languages. Figure 4.4 develops an awareness of language varieties and asks students to recognize and contrast the features of two linguistic systems.

Figure 4.4 Varieties of Language

Pronuciation

In the community	At school

Grammar Differences

In the community	At school

Vocabulary Terms

In the community	At school

Situation or Event

In the community	At school

#82: HIGH-PERFORMING TEACHERS OF HIGH-POVERTY STUDENTS

Haberman (1995) has identified the core behaviors of exemplary teachers of poor and disadvantaged students. In his 30 years of research, Haberman asserted that school reforms only take hold when they are supported by a system of pedagogy that is practiced schoolwide. He describes the characteristics of "star teachers" who have what it takes to help students succeed:

1. Star teachers are avid problem solvers. They seek to engage every student in learning—gifted, overlooked, academically challenged, or underserved. (Haberman, 1995, pp. 21-28)

2. Star teachers go beyond the traditional textbook by scanning current school, community, and world events and using such topics to capture student interest. They model a contagious love of learning. (pp. 29-41)

3. Star teachers use active learning processes and explain what they are doing and why. They point out the broad generalizations and concepts that undergird and connect daily lessons. (pp. 41-48)

4. Star teachers assume responsibility for all students and do not attribute academic underachievement to shortcomings in the students themselves, the schools, or society. (pp. 48-54)

5. Star teachers establish close and supportive relationships with students, not to satisfy their needs or preferences but to connect learning in ways that are meaningful for those they teach. (pp. 54-60)

6. Star teachers address bureaucratic demands by prioritizing what is necessary and what may be optional. They grow adept at clerical tasks and record keeping, attend important meetings (and forgo others), and learn how to advocate for students outside the classroom. (pp. 60-68)

7. Star teachers acknowledge their individual fallibility. They know they make mistakes, admit them, and work to correct and prevent them. (pp. 68-71)

8. Star teachers have emotional and physical stamina fueled by an inherent enthusiasm for what they do. Such qualities prevent burnout and keep them engaged in the dailiness of teaching. (pp. 71-73)

9. Star teachers have strong organizational and management skills, evident when using complex instructional methods, such as project-based learning, and when connecting the classroom with real-world experiences. (pp. 73-76)

10. Star teachers believe that success is derived from effort rather than chance or talent and communicate this belief to students. (pp. 76-78)

11. Star teachers distinguish between giving directions and providing instruction. They see teaching as interacting with students, not just giving explanations and expecting students independently to follow directions. They convey that the students and teacher are on the same side, the learning side, and that they are not pitted against each other. (pp. 79-82)

12. Star teachers communicate that students are valuable members of a learning community and that, without them, the group would not be complete. Instead of using coercion, such teachers create safe havens and demonstrate respect by creating an inclusive classroom climate. (pp. 83-86)

#83: REDUCING PREJUDICE BY INCREASING CRITICAL THINKING

Students can learn critical thinking skills that counteract prejudicial tendencies. Bias often emerges when students use faulty reasoning, such as overgeneralizing and not following thoughts to their logical conclusions. Cotton (1993, p. 6), in her work on fostering intercultural harmony, suggests that students can practice the following thinking skills as an antidote to bias and stereotyping.

Intellectual Curiosity

Seek answers to a wide variety of questions and problems. Consider the causes and explanations of events by asking who, what, why, when, and where.

Objectivity

Rely on evidence and valid arguments when making a decision.

Open-Mindedness

Consider numerous perspectives and beliefs as being simultaneously true.

Flexibility

Be willing to change your mind. Avoid rigid and dogmatic attitudes.

Healthy Skepticism

Be willing to reject a hypothesis until adequate evidence is available.

Intellectual Honesty

Accept a statement as true when the evidence warrants, even though it conflicts with a previously held belief.

Being Systematic

Follow a line of thinking to its logical conclusion. Stay on track when confronted by tangents or topics that are irrelevant.

Persistence

Pursue evidence and arguments to support a point of view.

Decisiveness

Be willing to arrive at a conclusion when there is adequate evidence.

Respect Other Viewpoints

Listen respectfully to other viewpoints and be willing to admit if you are wrong, and another's ideas seem correct.

#84: MULTICULTURAL MATH

Math is often presented as empirical and objective, devoid of cultural content. As a collection of logical, verifiable processes, math is a universal language. However, when viewed through cultural and social systems, it becomes evident that there are different ways of perceiving the world mathematically. A few suggestions for integrating multiculturalism into math instruction follow.

1. Address the evolution of mathematical vocabulary. Some examples to consider include the Arabic origin of the word *algebra*, the Babylonian concept of *sexagesimal* numerals yielding hours and minutes, and the Hindu concept of zero.

2. Consider different approaches to classification systems. For example, the Cree and Ojibwa tribes classify plants and animals according to their function rather than using the Western system that is based on structure.

3. Use a variety of counting and measurement tools. For example, training with the Japanese abacus can assist students in transferring concepts to paper and pencil computations. Coast Salish tribes in the northwestern United States had a measurement that extended from the thumb to the middle fingertip with the fingers outstretched. Students can learn to estimate with this form of measurement and then convert it into English and metric forms.

4. The concepts of fractions, ratio, and proportion can be reinforced by making recipes from other cultures and by calculating currencies from other countries.

5. Patterning and symmetry can be studied in the art and architecture of many cultures.

6. Maps of different countries can be used to teach distance and proportion, while their calendars can show different ways of tracking time.

7. Invite guest speakers to the classroom to talk about how they use mathematics in daily life. For example, relatives and community members introduced one sixth-grade class in the Southwest to the use of measurement, calculation, and fractions in the construction business.

8. The *World Almanac for Kids* (World Almanac, 2003) can serve as an excellent resource for percentages, statistical data, and graphing.

9. Students and guest speakers can teach one another multicultural games that use mathematical concepts.

#85: MULTICULTURAL LITERATURE

Multicultural literature can be used in the classroom to accomplish several important goals. Three include increasing the achievement of minority students, raising cultural awareness, and providing enrichment for all students. Much multicultural literature addresses the issue of identity and the interplay between defining ourselves through our differences from and commonalities with others. Since identity development is a primary task of adolescence, the following thematically organized literary suggestions target adolescents and support their efforts with identity formation (Brown & Stephens, 1998, pp. 35-100).

Connecting the Past With the Present

The book *The Diary of a Young Girl* by Anne Frank can be used to inspire memoir writing among immigrant (and all other) students. Discussions and writing assignments can address taking refuge, overcoming obstacles, lack of schooling, and longing for peace and stability.

Journeys

Selected books can be assigned to small groups of students who consider how journeys are portrayed and experienced by various literary characters. Such texts might include *Dogsong* by Gary Paulsen about an Alaskan Native boy's path to manhood; *Journey of the Sparrows* by Fran Leeper Buss about a family forced to flee El Salvador; and *Journey to Topaz* by Yoshiko Uchida about the internment of Japanese Americans during World War II.

Overcoming Obstacles

Persistence, effort, and positive attitudes are usually necessary ingredients in any success in life. Students can read one or more of the following books for inspiration to continue trying when the going gets tough: *Alicia, My Story* by Alicia Appleman-Jurman talks about surviving the Holocaust; *Winning* by Robin Brancato is about a star football player who becomes paralyzed after a tackle on the field; *Silver Rights* by Constance Curry recounts the desegregation of an all-white school in the South; and *The Story of My Life* by Helen Keller shows heroic efforts to live with deafness and blindness.

Writing One's Life

Rio Grande Stories by Carolyn Meyer demonstrates how students and teachers can successfully publish a book. A multicultural seventh-grade class in New Mexico researched their own heritages and wrote about how their communities live along the Rio Grande River. The book features the writing of Native American, Hispanic, African American, Anglo, and Jewish students and is an impressive model of how students can teach others about their cultures.

SUGGESTED READINGS FOR FURTHER INFORMATION

Banks, J., & Banks, C. (Eds.). (2001). *Multicultural Education: Issues and Perspectives* (4th ed.). New York: John Wiley.

This classic in the field of multicultural education introduces educators to issues of race, class, gender, language and religious diversity, and exceptionality, and the influence of such variables on student learning. Leading scholars define terms, present research, and address debates and controversies in the field. Topics include the evolution and characteristics of multicultural education, school and curricular reform, the limitations of color-blindness in the classroom, and numerous aspects of diversity. Also highlighted are classroom practices that successfully educate students from numerous backgrounds. This book is a must read for anyone who wants a broad grounding in multicultural education, its goals, challenges, and promises.

Ovando, C., & Collier, V. (1998). *Bilingual and ESL Classrooms: Teaching in Multicultural Contexts.* Boston: McGraw-Hill.

Since most teachers have little or no training in working with ELLs in the classroom, this book is a worthwhile addition to any personal or professional library. The authors describe the brief history of bilingual education, untangle the numerous controversies surrounding this field, and give teachers needed guidance in teaching language minority students in the classroom. The scope of the book is broad and considers student demographic data, language policy and programs, effective classroom practices for ESL and mainstream teachers, the role of culture in learning, teaching and assessing a variety of disciplines, and school and community collaboration.

Cole, R. W. (Ed.). (1995). *Educating Everybody's Children: Diverse Teaching Strategies for Diverse Learners.* Alexandria, VA: Association for Supervision and Curriculum Development.

Cole, R. W. (Ed.). (2001). *More Strategies for Educating Everybody's Children.* Alexandria, VA: Association for Supervision and Curriculum Development.

These two books provide research-derived principles for teaching in diverse classrooms. Each chapter addresses a specific aspect of diversity, such as immigrant children or those who are homeless, and is followed by descriptions of teaching strategies and their application in the classroom. The books pose the question, What might all children attempt if they knew they would not fail? and answers with the notion of a pedagogy of plenty rather than of poverty.

REFERENCES

Allington, R. L. (2001). *What really matters for struggling readers: Designing research-based programs.* New York: Longman.

Arroyo, A., Rhoad, R., & Drew, P. (1999, Summer). Meeting diverse student needs in urban schools: Research-based recommendations for school personnel. *Preventing School Failure, 43*(4), 145-153.

Association for Supervision and Curriculum Development. (2000, Summer). *Before it's too late: Giving reading a last chance* (curriculum update). Alexandria, VA: Author.

Baum, S., Renzulli, S., & Hebert, T. (1995). The prism metaphor: A new paradigm for reversing underachievement. *Gifted Child Quarterly, 39*(4), 224-235.

Brice, A., & Roseberry-McKibbin, C. (1999, April). Turning frustration into success for English language learners. *Educational Leadership, 56*(7), 53-55.

Brown, J. E., & Stephens, E. C. (Eds.). (1998). *United in diversity: Using multicultural young adult literature in the classroom.* Urbana, IL: National Council of Teachers of English.

Coates, R. D. (1989). The regular education initiative and opinions of regular classroom teachers. *Journal of Learning Disabilities, 22,* 532-536.

Collicott, J. (1991). Implementing multi-level instruction: Strategies for classroom teachers. In G. L. Porter & D. Richler (Eds.), *Changing Canadian schools: Perspectives on disability and inclusion* (pp. 191-218). Toronto, Ontario: G. Allen Roeher Institute.

Cotton, K. (1993). *Fostering intercultural harmony.* Portland, OR: Northwest Regional Educational Laboratory. Retrieved August 11, 2002, from www.nwrel.org/scpd/sirs/8/topsyn7.html

Diamond, B., & Moore, M. (1993). *Using multicultural literature to increase reading engagement and comprehension.* Retrieved August 2, 2002, from the Center for Multicultural Education, University of Washington, depts.washington.edu/centerme/mlp.htm#compo

Education for All Handicapped Children Act (1975). Pub. L. No. 94-142.

Educational Research Service. (2001). *Student mobility.* Arlington, VA: Author.

Elbaum, B., Moody, S., Vaughn, S., Schumm, J., & Hughes, M. (1999). The effects of instructional grouping format of students with disabilities: A meta-analytic review. *National Center for Learning Disabilities.* Retrieved August 2, 2002, from www.ncld.org/research/index.cfm

Frasier, M., & Passow, A. (1994). *Toward a new paradigm for identifying talent potential* [Monograph 94112]. Storrs, CT: National Research Center on the Gifted and Talented.

Gay, G. (2001). Educational equality for students of color. In J. A. Banks & C. M. Banks (Eds.), *Multicultural education: Issues and perspectives* (pp. 197-224). New York: John Wiley.

Gersten, R., Baker, S., Marks, S., & Smith, S. (1999). Effective instruction for learning disabled or at-risk English-language learners: An integrative synthesis of the empirical and professional knowledge bases. *National Center for Learning Disabilities.* Retrieved August 2, 2002, from www.ncld.org/research/index.cfm

Haberman, M. (1995). *Star teachers of children in poverty.* West Lafayettte, IN: Kappa Delta Pi.

Hallahan, D., & Kauffman, J. (1994). From mainstreaming to collaborative consultation. In J. Kauffman & D. Hallahan (Eds.), *The illusion of full inclusion* (pp. 3-17). Austin, TX: PRO-ED.

Idol, L., Nevin, A., & Paolucci-Whitcomb, P. (1994). *Collaborative consultation.* Austin, TX: PRO-ED.

Individuals With Disabilities Education Act Amendments (1997). Pub. L. No 105-17.

Johnson, G. M. (1999, Winter). Inclusive education: Fundamental instructional strategies and considerations. *Preventing School Failure, 43*(2), 72-78.

Joos, M. (1972). The styles of the five clocks. In R. Abrahams and R. Troike (Eds.), *Language and Cultural Diversity in American Education.* Englewood, NJ: Prentice Hall.

Legal Information Institute. (n.d.). *Stewart B. McKinney Homeless Assistance Act 1987.* Retrieved August 7, 2002, from www.4.law.cornell.edu/uscode/42/ch119.html

National Center for Children in Poverty. (2001). *Child poverty fact sheet: Child poverty in the United States.* Retrieved August 3, 2002, from cpmcnet.columbia.edu/dept/nccp/ycpf.html

National Center for Homeless Education. (n.d.). *Data on homeless children and youth.* Retrieved August 3, 2002, from www.serve.org/nche

National Clearinghouse for English Language Acquisition. (2002). *Elementary and secondary LEP enrollment growth and top languages.* Retrieved October 27, 2002 from: www.ncea.gwu.edu/index.html

Nelson-Legall, S. A. (1985). Help-seek behavior in Learning. In E. W. Gordon (Ed.). *Review of research in education.* Vol. 12, pp. 55-90. Washington, DC: American Educational Research Association.

Northwest Regional Educational Laboratory. (2001). *Meeting the needs of immigrant students.* Retrieved August 17, 2002, from www.nwrel.org/cnorse/booklets/immigration/index.html

Oakes, J. (1985). *Keeping track: How schools structure inequality.* New Haven, CT: Yale University Press.

Olson, M., Chalmers, L., & Hoover, J. (1997, January/February). Attitudes and attributes of general education teachers identified as effective inclusionists. *Remedial and Special Education, 18*(1), 28-35.

Ovando, C., & Collier, V. (1998). *Bilingual and ESL classrooms: Teaching in multicultural contexts.* Boston: McGraw-Hill.

Page, R. (1991). *Lower track classrooms: A curricular and cultural perspective.* New York: Teachers College Press.

Payne, R. (1995). *Poverty: A framework for understanding and working with students and adults from poverty.* Baytown, TX: RFT Publishing.

Pressley, M., Allington, R., Wharton-McDonald, R., Collins-Block, C., & Morrow, L. (2001). *Learning to read: Lessons from exemplary first-grade classrooms.* New York: Guilford.

Revilla, A. T., & Sweeney, Y. D. (1997). *High performing/high poverty schools.* Retrieved August 3, 2002, from the Intercultural Development Research Association, www.starcenter.org/documents/lowincome.htm

Schumm, J. S., Vaughn, S., & Sobol, M. C. (1997, January). Are they getting it? How to monitor student understanding in inclusive classrooms. *Intervention in School and Clinic, 32*(3), 168-171.

Slavin, R. (1987). Ability grouping and student achievement in the elementary schools: A best evidence synthesis. *Review of Educational Research, 57,* 293-336.

Snow, C., Burns, S., & Griffin, P. (1998). *Preventing reading difficulties in young children.* Washington, DC: National Academy Press.

Subotnik, R., & LeBlanc, G. (2001). Teaching gifted students in a multicultural society. In J. A. Banks & C. M. Banks (Eds.), *Multicultural education: Issues and perspectives* (pp. 353-376). New York: John Wiley.

Thomas, W. P., & Collier, V. P. (1997). School effectiveness for language minority students. Washington, DC: *National Clearinghouse for Bilingual Education.*

U.S. Census Bureau. (2001). *Poverty: 2000 highlights.* Retrieved August 3, 2002, from www.census.gov/hhes/poverty/poverty00/pov00hi.html

U.S. Department of Education. (1997a). *America reads challenge: Evidence that tutoring works.* Retrieved August 3, 2002, from www.ed.gov/inits/americareads/resourcekit/miscdocs/tutorwork.html

U.S. Department of Education. (1997b). *Assessment of student performance: Studies of educational reform.* Retrieved August 3, 2002, from www.ed.gov/pubs/SER/ASP/

U.S. Department of Education, National Center for Educational Statistics. (1998). *Statistical analysis report: State survey on racial and ethnic classifications.* Retrieved August 3, 2002, from nces.ed.gov/pubsearch/pubsinfo.asp?pubid=98034

U.S. Department of Education, National Center for Educational Statistics. (2001a). *Overview of public elementary and secondary schools and districts: School year 1999-2000.* Retrieved August 3, 2002, from nces.ed.gov/pubs2001/overview/

U.S. Department of Education, National Center for Educational Statistics. (2001b). Public school student, staff and graduate counts by state: School year 1999-2000. *Education Statistics Quarterly.* Retrieved August 3, 2002, from nces.ed.gov/pubsearch/getpubList.asp?L1=101&L2=4

U.S. Department of Education, National Center for Educational Statistics. (n.d.). *National assessment of educational progress: Reading.* Retrieved August 9, 2002, from nces.ed.gov/nationalreportcard/reading

U.S. Department of Education, National Institute for Literacy. (2000). *Reading: Know what works.* Washington, DC: Author.

U.S. Department of Education, Office of Special Education and Rehabilitative Services. (2000). *Twenty-second annual report to congress on the implementation of the Individuals with Disabilities Education Act.* Retrieved August 3, 2002, from www.ed.gov/offices/OSERS/OSEP/Products/OSEP2000AnlRpt/

Vissing, Y. M. (1996). *Out of sight, out of mind.* Lexington: University Press of Kentucky.

Webb, M. (1990). Multicultural education in elementary and secondary schools. *ERIC Digest #67.* Retrieved August 3, 2002, from www.ed.gov/databases/ ERIC_Digests/ed327613.html

Wheelock, A. (1992). *Crossing the tracks: How untracking can save America's schools.* New York: New Press.

World Almananc (Ed.). (2003). *World almanac for kids.* New York: World Almanac Books.

5

Assessing Student Performance

During the last two decades, the limitations of multiple-choice, matching, and true-or-false tests have caused educators to develop assessment alternatives. In classrooms across the country, teachers now use journals, presentations, portfolios, essays, and rubrics to assess student learning. More than ever before, assessment is regarded as an integrated component of the instructional process rather than an end-of-unit activity. This dissolution of the boundaries between teaching and assessing reflects broader educational shifts. Students are no longer perceived as passive recipients of information. They are active participants in their learning and, in many cases, are called on to actively demonstrate what they have learned.

As with any other aspect of education, assessment is a complex issue and one that evokes considerable debate. Rather than focus on controversies about standardized testing, this chapter maintains that data gathered from numerous sources can improve learning and teaching. Recent research, in fact, shows that new assessment procedures and varied uses of assessment data positively influence student learning (Black & Wiliam, 1998; DuFour, 2000; Educational Research Service, 2001; Massell, 2000; Schmoker, 2001; Stiggins, 1994; U.S. Department of Education, 1997).

For example, when teachers review individual student and whole group responses to state level tests, they can identify those skills that were learned and those that require additional attention. This information can be acted on to support students who might otherwise fall behind and to advance those who possess a thorough grasp of the content. Likewise, classroom performance assessments often lead to changes in instruction and student achievement

(Black & Wiliam, 1998; Stiggins, 1994, 2000; U.S. Department of Education, 1997; Wiggins, 2000; Wiggins & McTighe, 1998). Teachers reported that performance assessments changed their teaching practices, increased student motivation, and resulted in greater achievement gains. Some also claimed that performance measures more equitably assess the performance of ethnic minority and language minority students (North Central Regional Educational Laboratory, 1997).

In the literature on assessment, there are conflicting terms, purposes, and processes. This chapter establishes a common frame of reference by defining concepts, clarifying the purposes of assessment, and describing 15 strategies. The concept of assessment used in this book is broader than that of assigning grades to students. It is perceived as an ongoing reflective process that involves collecting, synthesizing, and interpreting information about students' learning and teachers' teaching. Classroom assessment serves several key purposes. These are

- To gather data about students' background knowledge
- To monitor learning
- To give students feedback during and after instruction
- To promote growth
- To recognize accomplishment
- To evaluate achievement
- To inform parents and the broader community about student learning
- To improve instruction
- To modify a program

It is helpful to be clear about the purposes of assessment, since all purposes are not necessarily compatible with one another. Emphasis on one purpose, such as end-of-the-term evaluative assessments, may not necessarily lead to enhanced pedagogy. It is unlikely that any one assessment will serve all purposes well. What is important is to match assessment purposes with the appropriate tasks. In general, most effective classroom practices typically require a blend of three types of assessment: diagnostic, formative, and summative. These and other terms are defined below.

DEFINING ASSESSMENT TERMS

The field of assessment is replete with disagreements about the meaning of terms. Since there are literally no universally accepted definitions, those that follow have been culled and distilled from many sources. Just as these definitions serve as a starting point for this chapter, it is important when teachers discuss assessment in their buildings that they define the terms they discuss.

Alternative assessment. This broad concept refers to any type of assessment in which students create responses to questions instead of responding to a prepared list of responses such as in multiple-choice, true-false, or matching questions. Sample alternative assessments include short-answer questions, essays, performances, oral presentations, and portfolios.

Assessment. Assessment is the process of quantifying, describing, or gathering data, or giving feedback to others about what a learner knows and can do. Assessment results in identifying instructional practices that could be improved and supplying different resources for students. Various methods can be used to obtain information about student learning to guide decisions and actions. Some include observations, interviews, projects, tests, performances, and portfolios.

Authentic assessment. Authentic assessment is the process of gathering evidence or documenting a student's learning in ways that resemble real life, such as a driving test, a presentation, or addressing a community problem.

Diagnostic assessment. Diagnostic assessment typically occurs at the beginning of a unit of study or term. It involves identifying prior knowledge, using such strategies as those in Chapter 1, and is used to identify student difficulties, strengths, and interests and to make informed decisions about where to focus instruction.

Evaluation. Evaluation is the process of interpreting and making judgments about the quality, value, or worth of a response, product, or performance. Such judgments are usually based on preestablished criteria.

Formative assessment. Formative assessment occurs frequently during teaching and learning. It provides ongoing diagnostic information to teachers about instructional effectiveness and to students about the status of their learning. Formative assessment occurs when teachers and students reflect on learning, give feedback, practice to improve skills, set goals, and make adjustments to teaching and learning.

Performance assessment. Performance assessments contrast with true-or-false and multiple-choice tasks by asking students to construct responses, create products, or perform demonstrations to provide evidence of what they know and can do.

Portfolio. A portfolio is a purposeful collection of products and criteria that demonstrates students' growth in knowledge and skill over time.

Reporting. Reporting consists of sharing information about student learning and often consists of evaluative judgments.

Rubric. A rubric is a set of scoring criteria used to guide and evaluate student work. Rubrics provide descriptive levels for performance, such as exemplary, competent, or novice.

Summative assessment. Summative assessment typically occurs at the end of a chapter, unit, course, grade level, or series of courses. It provides feedback to students, parents, and higher-education institutions about progress and achievement. Summative assessment typically leads to a status report on a student's degree of proficiency, and judgments are made according to preestablished criteria. It is often used by others to make decisions about appropriate placement and helps students decide about further study. It is a snapshot of student achievement at a given time.

WHAT DOES THE
RESEARCH SAY ABOUT
USING ASSESSMENT TO IMPROVE
TEACHING AND LEARNING?

Assessment appears most beneficial when it is an integrated part of the instructional cycle. Teachers can plan for assessment just as they plan for instruction. In fact, many suggest that teachers plan backward (Hibbard & Yakimowski, 1997; Wiggins & McTighe, 1998) by identifying the desired results they hope to attain first, then determining acceptable evidence and planning learning experiences. Prior to teaching new content, diagnostic forms of assessment are helpful in determining students' level of knowledge (Bransford, Brown, & Cocking, 1999). Once instruction has begun, effective assessment practices include those that are aligned with curricular goals, collect student data over time, include active student participation, sample a range of skills and competencies, use a variety of approaches, and are teacher designed (U.S. Department of Education, 1997). Many studies also emphasize the value of formative assessment, since it plays an important role in shaping teaching and learning (Black & Wiliam, 1998; Wiggins & McTighe, 1998).

Recent research has revealed that performance assessment positively influences classrooms in four key areas: curriculum development, instruction, teacher roles, and student roles. For example, portfolios influence curriculum by forgoing breadth of coverage for depth of coverage (U.S. Department of Education, 1997). Many teachers use scoring rubrics to set performance standards and expectations. Such rubrics, when explained prior to beginning work, increase students' awareness of expectations and establish a frame of reference for judging their work and that of their peers. Student complaints about grades have been shown to decrease when the criteria are explicit (U.S. Department of Education, 1997). Furthermore, reflecting on specific assessment data spotlights students who struggle with content. With an increased awareness of achievement targets, teachers can help students meet expectations. For example, the failure rate in some cases was diminished through adding focused study time and a new class in math (Feldman & Tung, 2001).

Reducing the reliance on textbook-based assignments and tests changes the nature of instruction, too. When teachers assign performance-based tasks, student learning typically expands to include writing, content knowledge, and problem solving (U.S. Department of Education, 1997). The increase in writing across the curriculum has yielded gains in students' writing skills. Performance tasks also foster analytic thinking. Students must actively seek, structure, and communicate information to others and, in so doing, use a wide variety of thinking and communication skills.

Increased use of formative types of assessment has been linked with significant achievement gains. In a review of 250 studies, Black and Wiliam (1998) found that formative assessment, often simply in the form of advice or feedback, benefited students at all ability levels, while grading did not result in improved work.

Another instructional change brought about by performance assessment is increased collaboration among students (Feldman & Tung, 2001; Seidel, 1991; U.S. Department of Education, 1997). Presentations, exhibits, or experiments are often conducted by small groups of students. Additionally, the use of rubrics increases opportunities for peer assessment, since students know the targets for their learning and can self-assess or give advice to classmates.

Teacher roles have also transformed with performance assessment. Teachers become more reflective about their practices (Feldman & Tung, 2001), and collaboration with colleagues increases. More collaboration occurs because teachers seek out peers to discuss details about performance assessment and to analyze portfolios that span multiple grades or levels or subjects. The U.S. Department of Education (1997) found that teacher creativity was enhanced through efforts to assign multiple forms of performance assessment.

Classroom assessment, and especially the use of performance-based measures, can make a critical difference in student learning (Black & Wiliam, 1998; Ulmer, 2001; U.S. Department of Education, 1997). Students exhibited a greater motivation when working on performance tasks and portfolio assignments than with traditional types of textbook-based assignments. Both teachers and students attributed this engagement to the sustained attention and effort such assignments necessitated. Likewise, students have demonstrated good research and presentation skills through project-based assessment.

Many teachers ask students to participate in establishing assessment criteria and to self-assess their work. Student learning has benefited from this active participation (Pike, 1995; Seidel, 1991). Furthermore, when students are involved in their own assessment, they have opportunities to think about their learning. They become responsible for determining whether they are learning and understanding content. Self-assessment, whether through journals or portfolios, helps students internalize academic goals, think critically, and become independent learners (Davison & Pearce, 1992).

In addition to determining whether students are achieving academically, assessment can be used to identify the nonacademic intangibles in the classroom (Nelson, 2000). Such intangibles might include a student's daily attendance, ability to engage socially in positive ways, and impulse control. Frequently, teachers notice changes in students, but such changes aren't easily measured. According to Nelson (2000), teachers can document five categories of nonacademic behavior: (a) attendance; (b) classroom participation such as asking appropriate questions, participating in small groups, and transferring learning to other situations; (c) attentiveness as demonstrated through on-task behavior; (d) social skills; and (e) classroom behaviors. Recording these five areas, as shown later in this chapter, can provide helpful information to students, parents, and colleagues. The areas serve as indicators of interpersonal and intrapersonal growth and can signal academic opportunities.

USING PERFORMANCE ASSESSMENT IN THE CLASSROOM

Research indicates that assessment can move from reflecting on learning to enhancing learning. This shift occurs when teachers are explicit about what students should know, when multiple assessment measures are used over time, when tangibles as well as intangibles are considered, and when students are active self-assessors. The strategies in this chapter dissolve traditional lines between learning and assessment and support the development of positive assessment cultures in classrooms.

The pages that follow address a variety of assessment issues. These include planning for assessment, identifying assessment criteria, and techniques for taking standardized tests—a reality for nearly every student. Formative assessment processes are emphasized throughout. As a result, there are learning logs, anecdotal records, observation guides, oral classroom assessment, and interviews. Significantly, students are taught how to assess themselves. With an ability to direct and redirect their effort, students and teachers together can achieve a major goal of education—learning how to learn and how to improve one's learning.

#86: IT'S NOT BUSINESS AS USUAL: PLANNING FOR ASSESSMENT

To begin improving assessment, it is helpful to be intentional about how and why we teach the content we do and whether students will learn from our efforts. Some guiding questions answered at the outset of a new unit of study can ensure that learning is productive from start to finish.

Before Instruction

- Why do I include this content in what I teach?
- What will students know by the end of this unit?
- How does this content support the course's outcomes, the state's standards, or other goals?
- What do students already know about this material? How can I find out?
- How can I make my goals for learning clear?
- How should I inform students of the learning targets to be met?
- What evidence will show that students have learned the content?
- What instructional strategies do I plan to use?
- What adaptations might I need to make for individuals or groups?

During Instruction

- What advice can I give to help students?
- What kinds of feedback can students give each other?
- Who is stuck, and what can I do to jump start their learning?
- How can I have students reflect on their thinking and modify it?
- How might students support each other in meeting the learning targets?

After Instruction

- How did students perform overall?
- How did they perform on specific objectives?
- How did different subgroups of students perform, such as those who are highly mobile or in a language minority?
- Why did they perform at that level?
- What can be done to improve their performance?
- How can I engage students in self-reflection about their learning?
- What remediation is needed and for whom?

#87: BEGINNING WITH THE END IN MIND

Planning for instruction is like planning a trip. The destination is identified first, the route and means of travel are determined, and the stops along the way are also mapped out. Of course, interesting and unplanned detours can occur, but people usually arrive at their desired destination somewhat on schedule and know how they got there. Planning instruction backward by specifying the desired results first, the acceptable evidence second, and the learning experiences third can help orient teachers and students to the journey ahead. The questions in Figure 5.1 guide the planning process.

Figure 5.1 Planning Worksheet

What important concepts or big picture ideas should students know?
(Examples: large concepts, theories, or principles, such as human rights in a democracy, how personal identity is addressed in literature, or the ability of the arts to mirror and lead culture)

What evidence will reveal that students understand? (Examples: projects, essays, quizzes, presentations, observations, and student self-assessment)

How will students know where they are headed? (Examples: rubrics, completed samples, and grading criteria)

What teaching and learning experiences will assist students in acquiring the targeted learnings? (Examples: sequence of instruction or learning activities)

_____

_____

_____

How will progress be gauged during instruction? (Examples: informal observations, teacher and student feedback, discussions)

_____

_____

_____

How will student learning be demonstrated? (Examples: performances and products)

_____

_____

_____

How will students self-assess? (Examples: debriefings, comparison of one's work against the rubric, journal entries)

_____

_____

_____

SOURCE: Adapted from G. Wiggins & J. McTighe (1998, pp. 81-186).

#88: TAKING STOCK: STUDENT SELF-ASSESSMENT

Students can learn to self-assess at young ages. Self-assessment helps students to internalize the learning goals, to identify the strengths and weaknesses of their work, and to manage their individual learning. Such processes can begin in the early grades. Figure 5.2A is an example of a primary-level rubric.

With older students, a summative self-assessment might look like the one in Figure 5.2B.

Figure 5.2A   Self-Rating for Younger Students

Name: _____   Date: _____

On this assignment, I think my work is:

4 = Super! This is my best work.

3 = Well done. I made good effort.

2 = OK. I could have done better. Ideas I have to improve this are:

1 = Not very good. I would like to redo this work. I need help with:

Figure 5.2B   Self-Rating for Older Students

Name: _____

What key ideas did you learn from this unit?

_____

_____

_____

_____

_____

What did you learn about yourself from working on this assignment?

_____

_____

_____

_____

_____

What are the strengths of this assignment?

_____

_____

_____

_____

_____

What could be done to improve your work?

_____

_____

_____

_____

_____

Does this assignment meet the specified criteria? How or why not?

_____

_____

_____

_____

#89: COLLABORATIVE-ASSESSMENT CONFERENCES

Collaborative-assessment conferences, as developed by Seidel (1991), involve students and teachers in conversations about the quality of significant student work. Such conferences democratize the assessment process by giving those who will be assessed the opportunity to say what assessment should look like. Assessment conferences are usually conducted both before students start work on a major assignment and after they have completed it. The conferences are based on the assumption that serious student work deserves serious teacher and student response and attention.

First Conference: Establishing Assessment Criteria

Before embarking on an important assignment or project, teachers and students can collaboratively identify the criteria for assessing the completed work. During 30 or so minutes of discussion, both content and skill criteria can be identified and refined. For example, students might suggest that their work exhibit a clear understanding of a concept and that their knowledge be displayed visually or extended into real-world applications. The acceptable levels of proficiency can also be identified. During the first collaborative assessment conference, teachers also might show samples of previous student work so the class can consider whether such models met the criteria and why or why not.

Second Conference: Assessing Student Work

The second collaborative assessment conference is scheduled when assignments are due. Its intent is to showcase student work while also discussing how effectively the assignments met the preestablished criteria. Such conferences can be held individually, in small groups, or with the entire class. Guidelines follow for conducting this summative assessment process.

Discussion Guidelines

1. Ask students to explain their work, its quality, and what they learned.

2. In respectful, nonevaluative terms, describe the student's work.

3. Identify the most striking or noticeable features of the work. Ask whether the student has additional comments to make.

4. Ask questions about the work, and encourage classmates to do likewise.

5. Evaluate whether the work fulfills the preestablished criteria.

In closing the assessment conference, identify strengths evident in the assignment that could be extended to other work, and end on a positive note or with encouragement for future efforts.

#90: TEST-TAKING MATTERS

Standardized tests are likely here to stay. The skills they require can be taught and practiced by integrating them into common classroom assessments. Teachers can model how they would use each skill and in so doing demystify high-stakes test procedures while showing students how to do the following when taking a test:

1. Follow directions, including oral and written directions, and complex ones with multiple steps.

2. Respond to prompts by understanding what key terms mean, such as *summarize, give an example,* or *show your work.*

3. Practice using a variety of test formats.

4. Use answer sheets to find and mark the answer choices appropriately.

5. Manage time effectively by skipping difficult items to return to them later, allotting time to different segments of a test, and avoiding rushing.

6. Consider each answer choice by scanning for quick answers, making a good guess, eliminating incorrect options, determining when correct answers are not given, and checking one's choice.

7. Predict answers before considering options.

8. Refer to a passage to search for an answer.

9. Use key words, numbers, or graphs to solve problems.

10. Compute carefully.

#91: TEST-TAKING RULES FOR STUDENTS

1. Be excited to show what you know and can do!
2. Plan your time and pace yourself.
3. Read carefully, and ask yourself questions about what you are reading.
4. Follow directions.
5. Estimate an answer before looking at options.
6. Skip hard questions and answer easy questions first.
7. Know when and how to guess—eliminate obviously wrong answers and choose from among the best.
8. For writing tests, organize thoughts first and write in complete sentences.
9. Check your answers.
10. Use positive self-talk to complete the test with your best effort.

#92: GETTING TO KNOW YOU: ENTRY INTERVIEWS

Teachers can establish baseline data about student knowledge at the beginning of a unit or term by using diagnostic forms of assessment. One approach is to briefly interview students about a particular discipline. Older students or instructional aides can conduct the interviews and record responses, or students can use the forms as surveys to complete. Reflecting on the completed data gives teachers insight into the beginning knowledge and attitudes of those they are about to teach. Here is an example of a form for an entry interview (Campbell, Campbell, & Dickinson, 1999, p. 328):

Student name: _____ Date:_____

Subject or class: _____

Interviewer name: _____

- Is there someone you know well who has a strong interest in this subject or topic?

- If so, how do you know that person is interested in this topic?

- What have you learned from that person about this topic? Or, where have you encountered this topic before?

- What are one or two things you know about this topic?

- What is one thing you would like to learn?

- How do you think you could use this information in school? Outside of school?

- How do you learn best? What could the teacher do to make this topic interesting?

#93: SAYING GOODBYE: EXIT INTERVIEWS

In contrast to entry interviews, exit interviews ask teachers and students to reflect on what was learned, how it was learned, and what might be next. A sample exit interview form follows (Campbell, Campbell, & Dickinson, 1999, p. 309).

Student name: _____ Date:_____

Subject or class: _____

Interviewer's name: _____

1. Reflect on your earliest work in this class or on this topic. What are two or three key ideas you learned?

2. What did you learn that was new to you?

3. What did you most enjoy about the unit or course?

4. What problems did you encounter during the unit?

5. What did you learn about yourself as a learner from this class?

6. How can you use the information gained from this experience?

7. What grade do you think you deserve and why?

8. How have you changed because of this new knowledge?

9. What would like to learn next?

10. How would you get started?

#94: TAKING NOTE
WITH ANECDOTAL RECORDS

Anecdotal records are brief notes that describe significant behaviors during observations. When they are collected and reviewed over time, they help teachers perceive patterns of learning and behavior, make instructional decisions, and give students feedback. There are many ways to organize this type of formative assessment. Some teachers make generic grids that are filed in notebooks alphabetically by student names. Some use notebooks for each subject area, others use note cards that are filed, and some use Post-it notes that are later added to a student's file. A sample anecdotal record is in Figure 5.3.

Figure 5.3 Anecdotal Record of Significant Behavior

Student name: Deloria

Subject: Fifth-grade math

1/12 After students were asked to plan a trip budget, Deloria looked out the window, sharpened her pencil, and asked to go to the bathroom. When she returned, she participated in making a draft budget.

1/16 Deloria spent the first few minutes of class asking for supplies and getting organized. She completed most problems individually.

1/24 Deloria had difficulty getting started during the first 10 minutes of class today but seemed to benefit from my restating the directions to her.

1/2 Observation: Assist Deloria with being prepared to start tasks on time.

SOURCE: Adapted from K. Pike & S. Salend (1995, p. 16).

#95: MAKING RUBRICS

Rubrics are evaluative tools that describe the components of an assignment and levels for performance, such as novice, practitioner, and expert. They provide clear information to students and others about performance expectations and when students can assist in their development by suggesting the indicators of a quality performance. Establishing the contents of a rubric requires analysis of the specific material to be assessed and what responses might look like. Students can be involved in determining the characteristics of work at various levels of quality. The following guide assists in determining what student responses might look like at different score levels:

What would best-quality responses look like? List the characteristics below.

_____

_____

_____

_____

_____

_____

How many levels of performance are anticipated (3, 4, 5)? What would work look like at various levels? List the characteristics below.

5. _____

4. _____

3. _____

2. _____

1. _____

0. _____

Once a rubric is created, the individual students, their peers, and the teacher can all use the same form to provide feedback about the quality of any individual assignment. It is often interesting to see how opinions vary and why.

Figure 5.4 shows a sample rubric for assessing a piece of student writing. It includes spaces for the student to self-assess and to receive a classmate's and teacher's assessment.

Figure 5.4 Assessment of Student's Writing

Student name: _____

N = Novice—student's work shows emerging skills and knowledge.

A = Apprentice—student's work uses knowledge and skills adequately.

E = Exemplary—student's work is polished and error free.

Criterion	Novice	Apprentice	Exemplary	Self	Peer	Teacher
Writing conventions	Numerous errors in spelling, punctuation, or paragraphing.	A few errors in spelling, punctuation or paragraphing. Some editing required.	Consistently correct spelling, punctuation, or paragraphing. Adds original touches.			
Sentence structure	Sentences are incomplete, rambling, choppy, or awkward.	Sentences have adequate structure but little variety.	Sentences flow, are varied and creative.			
Vocabulary	Limited vocabulary. Lack of imagery or examples.	Ordinary language is used and conveys message but without imagery.	Word choice is interesting, with vivid images and creative expression.			
Ideas and content	Lacks focus.	Clear and focused writing.	Clear and focused writing that is engaging.			

#96: ASSESSING ORALLY

Think alouds, or *oral defenses* as Nunley (2000, p. 6) calls them, are brief student-teacher interactions in which students are asked to explain their thinking or learning during class time. Teachers can check in with each student at least once every 2 days by moving around the class and posing questions one-on-one. Such formative oral assessments short-circuit student misconceptions or confusion and prevent them from slipping through proverbial classroom cracks. Sample one-on-one assessment questions follow:

1. How would you rephrase my directions?

2. How will you start this task?

3. What is the next step you would take?

4. Tell me how you arrived at that decision.

5. Explain that idea.

6. How would you define that?

7. Can you explain this answer?

8. Compare this part of your work with this criterion on the rubric.

9. Can you give another example of that?

10. How could you improve your thinking about this?

#97: OBSERVATION LOGS

On a daily basis, teachers observe students' academic and behavioral interactions. Usually, such observations are informal and rarely documented. However, with intentional use, observations can yield important insights. Some teachers structure observations by setting aside a portion of a day for such activities or by planning to observe designated skills or specific students. Observations can also be unstructured by simply jotting down significant student events or behaviors. Teachers can develop generic observation guides that readily accommodate their goals. It is often helpful to make accompanying narrative comments (see Figure 5.5).

Figure 5.5 Observation Checklist

Class: _____ Date: _____

Ratings:

N = There is no evidence that student knows or uses the skill.

B = Student is beginning to use the skill.

P = Student is making progress in developing the skill.

C = Student displays competence.

Student Names	Target Skill:	Target Skill:	Narrative Comments
1.			
2.			
3.			
4.			
5.			

#98: CHECKING THEIR LISTS: STUDENT CHECKLISTS

Students can gauge their skill development against predetermined criteria displayed on simple checklists. When given the opportunity to do so, they can analyze, describe, and evaluate their learning experiences, successes, and challenges. The checklist in Figure 5.6 targets reading skills.

Figure 5.6 Student Self-Assessment of Reading Skills

Name: _____ Date: _____

Reading Skills	Never	Sometimes	Often
I enjoy reading.			
I ask myself questions when I read.			
I can summarize what I read.			
I take notes or highlight when I read.			

Reading Skills	Never	Sometimes	Often
I use other words, or the context, to understand a new word.			
I make graphic organizers of what I read.			
I talk with others about my reading.			
I connect what I read to my life.			
I write about what I read.			

#99: LEARNING LOGS

Learning logs can accomplish several learning and assessment goals. They encourage students to write and reason simultaneously, and they reflect growth over time. They can serve as diagnostic, formative, or summative assessment tools. Those students who have difficulty writing can maintain an audio log by tape-recording their reflections. Since the quality of students' writing can be enhanced with framed prompts, several are offered below:

1. Explain what you liked about the lesson today.

2. Define a key concept in your own words.

3. Write about what you didn't like today.

4. Explain how you arrived at a solution to the problem.

5. At the end of class today, write about what you learned, what was confusing, and what help you'd like to receive.

6. Defend your opinion about . . .

7. Connect what we are studying with something in the news or in your life.

8. Describe how you would teach a concept to someone you know.

9. Identify ways to improve this learning experience.

10. Evaluate an assignment or project against the specified criteria and arrive at a defensible grade.

#100: ASSESSING NONTRADITIONAL RESULTS

At times, it is helpful to have data to report student improvement in areas other than grades. It can make a difference to students, parents, and administrators to be able to explain, for example, that a student's attendance has improved by 40% over last semester, that complaints from others about behavior problems have decreased by one third in the last month, or that the student is asking at least three worthwhile questions weekly. Figure 5.7 is adapted from the work of Nelson (2000), who recommends that a teacher track a student's behavior for 2 days a week only (in this figure, Tuesdays and Thursdays), so that attention isn't diverted from others in the classroom.

Figure 5.7 Nontraditional Assessment of Student

Student: _____ Month: _____

Absences: _____ Referrals: _____ Tardies: _____

Social Behaviors	T	Th	T	Th	T	Th	T	Th
Negative (impulsive, disruptive, bullying, etc.)								
Positive (appropriate, supportive, helpful, etc.)								
Engagement								
Negative (apathetic, off task, uninterested, etc.)								
Positive (attentive, makes effort, asks questions, etc.)								
Reactions From Others								
Negative (complaints, infractions, avoidance, etc.)								
Positive (compliments, perceived as positive leader)								

SOURCE: Adapted from K. Nelson (2000).

#101: SCHEDULING ASSESSMENT

Teachers typically spend a great deal of time planning a quarter-, trimester-, or semester-long curriculum. The same kind of planning can lead to the development of a comprehensive assessment calendar. Teachers can occasionally step back and reflect on the timing and types of assessment that are most appropriate for their curricular goals. The schedule in Figure 5.8 is suggested as one possible model and features diagnostic, formative, and summative forms of assessment. Each item could serve as one entry into a student portfolio to reveal growth over time through multiple measures.

Figure 5.8 Assessment Calendar

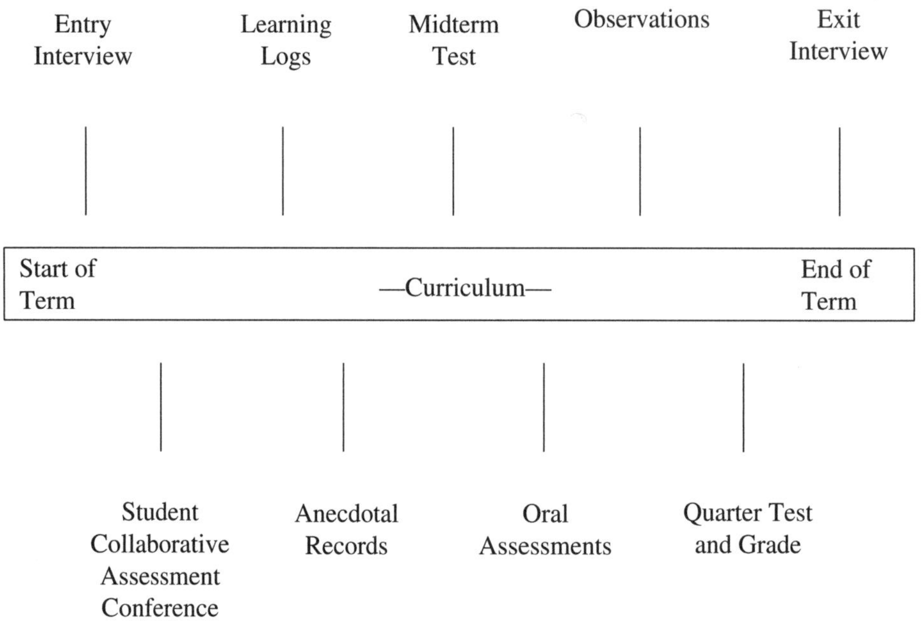

SOURCE: L. Campbell, B. Campbell, & D. Dickinson (1999, p. 327).

SUGGESTED READINGS
FOR FURTHER INFORMATION

Stiggins, R. (2000). *Student-Involved Classroom Assessment.* Upper Saddle River, NJ: Prentice Hall.

This book describes how to conduct daily assessment and how to use assessment to benefit students. It offers practical information on developing a variety of assessment tools, ways to match learning goals with assessment methods, and how to communicate assessment results. Stiggins also emphasizes the well-being of students in an assessment culture by emphasizing the important role of student self-assessment.

Wiggins, G. (2000). *Educative Assessment: Designing Assessments to Inform and Improve Student Performance.* San Francisco: Jossey-Bass.

For those interested in a new vision of assessment and its role in the classroom, this book provides helpful insights. Wiggins describes how to design performance-based assessments for use in curriculum and instruction—and as tools of broader educational reform. An important emphasis in the book is the how and why of providing ongoing, useful feedback so students gain knowledge and skills and in-depth understanding of worthwhile concepts.

Wiggins, G., & McTighe, J. (1998). *Understanding by Design.* Alexandria, VA: Association for Supervision and Curriculum Development.

Although it does not address assessment exclusively, this book explains backward curricular design that starts with identifying desired learning results. Wiggins and McTighe suggest that before planning curriculum, teachers step back to consider (a) what they want students to learn and understand, (b) what forms of evidence would document whether such learning was attained, and (c) appropriate learning experiences and instruction. Performance assessments naturally emerge within the context of meaningful learning.

REFERENCES

Black, P., & Wiliam, D. (1998, October). Inside the black box: Raising standards through classroom assessment. *Phi Delta Kappan, (80)*2, 139-159.

Bransford, J. D., Brown, A. L., & Cocking, R. R. (Eds.). (1999). *How people learn: Brain, mind, experience, and school.* Washington, DC: National Academy Press.

Campbell L., Campbell, B., & Dickinson, D. (1999). *Teaching and learning through multiple intelligences.* Needham Heights, MA: Allyn & Bacon.

Davison, D. M., & Pearce, D. L. (1992). The influence of writing activities on the mathematics learning of Native American students. *The Journal of Educational Issues of Language Minority Students, 10,* 147-157.

DuFour, R. (2000, Winter). Data put a face on shared vision. *Journal of Staff Development, 21*(1), 71-72.

Educational Research Service. (2001). *Student mobility.* Arlington, VA: Author.

Feldman, J., & Tung, R. (2001, Summer). Using data-based inquiry and decision-making to improve instruction. *ERS Spectrum: Journal of School Research and Information,* pp. 10-19.

Hibbard, M., & Yakimowski, M. (1997). *Assessment in Connecticut: A partnership to improve student performance—connecting state-level assessment and classroom practices.* Cheshire, CT: Connecticut Association for Supervision and Curriculum Development.

Massell, D. (2000). *The district role in building capacity: Four strategies.* Retrieved August 10, 2002, from www.gse.upenn.edu/cpre/Publications/rb32.pdf

Nelson, K. (2000, February). Measuring the intangibles. *Classroom Leadership: A Newsletter for K-12 Classroom Teachers,* pp. 1, 8.

North Central Regional Educational Laboratory. (1997). *Critical issue: Ensuring equity with alternative assessments.* Retrieved August 3, 2002, from www.ncrel.org/sdrs/areas/issues/methods/assment/as800.htm

Nunley, K. (2000, February). In defense of oral defense. *Classroom Leadership: A Newsletter for K-12 Classroom Teachers,* p. 6.

Pike, K. (1995, Fall). A comparison of traditional and authentic assessments. *Teaching Exceptional Children,* pp. 15-20.

Pike, K., & Salend, S. (1995, Fall). Authentic assessment strategies: Alternatives to norm-referenced testing. *Teaching Exceptional Children,* pp. 15-20.

Schmoker, M. (2001). *The results fieldbook: Practical strategies from dramatically improved schools.* Alexandria, VA: Association for Supervision and Curriculum Development.

Seidel, S. (1991). *Collaborative assessment conferences for the consideration of project work* [working paper]. Cambridge, MA: Project Zero, Harvard Graduate School of Education.

Stiggins, R. J. (1994). *Student-centered classroom assessment.* New York: Merrill.

Stiggins, R. J. (2000). *Student-involved classroom assessment.* Upper Saddle River, NJ: Prentice Hall.

Ulmer, M. B. (2001, Spring). Self-grading for formative assessment in problem-based learning. *Academic Exchange Quarterly,* pp. 68-74.

U.S. Department of Education. (1997). *Assessment of student performance: Studies of educational reform.* Retrieved August 3, 2002, from www.ed.gov/pubs/SER/ASP/

Wiggins, G. (2000). *Educative assessment: Designing assessments to inform and improve student performance.* San Francisco: Jossey-Bass.

Wiggins, G., & McTighe, J. (1998). *Understanding by design.* Alexandria, VA: Association for Supervision and Curriculum Development.

6

Some Concluding Thoughts

When walking in the hallways of many schools in America, observers find that the complexity of teaching asserts itself. A quick visit to a classroom reveals students who are native to the local community and others who are new to the United States, those who have been at the school for two or more years and those who arrived yesterday or last week. In most classrooms, there is a complex interplay of whole group, small group, and individualized instruction. It is evident that many students learn through listening, hands-on activities, drawing, and physical movement. Some effortlessly engage in quick dialogue while others require wait time and struggle. Resource teachers, specialists, and classroom teachers collaborate to assist those who might benefit. When overhearing teachers' conversations, one registers lively discussions of state standards, assessment requirements, teachers' curricular interests, students' interests, community goals, and instructional strategies.

At the end of a school visit, impressions linger of the rich and daunting mix of student nationalities, languages, and academic levels, and the packed curriculum that must be taught during a few short months. Education is a daily 1,000-piece jigsaw puzzle. How does one begin to fit the pieces together?

It seems that we can start by learning about our students and their communities. Doing so will enable us to meet students where they are and to identify new levels for them to attain. We can develop curriculum that balances student and teacher interests with state standards. We can use effective teaching techniques, and, while doing so, continually assess students' needs to flexibly adjust our approaches. We can vary the difficulty and pacing of our lessons, our texts, the types of questions we ask, the kinds of everyday connections

173

made, and the assessments used so that students experience success. In short, we need to become knowledgeable about what works in the classroom.

To do so, teachers must become lifelong students of learning. While teaching students important skills, knowledge, and attitudes, it is necessary to model such attributes ourselves. As the daily demands of teaching increase, so too has available research on what works. We can get to know our students, read and reflect, collaborate, and then customize curriculum, instruction, and assessment, all the while tapping new forms of support to guide our efforts.

Teachers want thoughtful, engaged, and mindful students. All students are unique and deserve the opportunity to learn all that they can. When students become excited about learning, they are eager to learn more. The key to engagement is excellent instruction. In this book, excellent instruction is grounded in research on teaching. Such research explains the hows and whys of what works in the classroom. Fortunately, research on teaching is a growing body of literature that teachers can rely on to improve student learning and professional competence. Not all of the 101 strategies are necessarily new, but what is new is that they are substantiated by research and practice that demonstrates their worthiness of being included in a mindful teacher's classroom repertoire.

Index